DAVID B. TRIEMERT

GETTING APPROVED

Making The American Credit System Work for You

1990's EDITION

Library of Congress Catalog Card No. 89-090687

ISBN 0-942731-22-0

Trade Paperback Edition ISBN 0-942731-41-7 (1990) $12.95
Spoken-Word Audio Edition ISBN 0-942731-45-X (1990) $59.95
Audio Book Pack ISBN 0-942731-48-4 (1990) $18.95

Printed in the United States of America

10 9 8 7 6 5 4 3 2 1

Dedication

To my nieces and nephews Heather, Chris, Becky, Jon, Tina, Danny and Michael.

The future ahead of you is very bright and will be full of wonderful opportunities and challenges to pursue. Preserve your *"child-like spirit"* and let it act as a guide in all that you do or encounter in life.

Hold on tight to your *"dreams"* with a white-knuckle grip, for that's the only *"thing"* in life that will *"truely"* bring forth a steady flow of peace, joy, happiness and success in the years to come.

Dare to *"dream"* big dreams, dare to *"believe"* in your dreams and dare to *"develop the courage and put forth the effort"* necessary to turn them into a "reality!"

A life without a dream is
like a boat without an oar,
A life without a dream is
like an ocean without a shore.

A life that's shaped and formed
by dreams is worthy of the fight,
A life that's shaped and formed by
dreams requires "courage" more than "might."

When the "going gets tough" or your "wings get clipped"
let not your "passion for life" up and die,
For it's the same "struggle encountered" that makes up
"Lifes Winners"
That teaches the "Eagle" himself how to fly!

With love . . .

Unk

Contents

CONTENTS

Foreword

Getting Approved will provide you with all the knowledge and basic skills to avoid Getting Denied.

We are all too familiar with books that promise to teach us how to manage our personal credit. Quite frankly, a whole stable of these credit books deal with quick-patch strategies that range from the profoundly ridiculous to outright illegal.

"Getting Approved: Making The American Credit System Work For You" is a solutions book. It explores an extensive menu of common consumer credit problems, and offers an excellent blend of conventional solutions and street-smart wisdom. It is designed for the novice trying to establish credit, those who need to re-establish credit, and for those who seek more advanced uses of their credibility.

David Triemert has succeded in creating an outstanding how-to credit book that is sensitive to the basic needs of the American consumer. His experience as an entrepreneur and credit consultant is reflected in the intricate details by which he dissects the inner workings of the American consumer credit system.

The labor invested in this book is a showcase of David's extensive interest in personal finance and concern for thousands of readers. A dilligent worker, tough negotiator and skillful dealmaker, David's work is truly impressive, with a style that makes for an easy reading.

Having read Getting Approved more than once is a delight worth sharing. As a client and a colleague, I am grateful to David for helping me improve my own credit profile and for extending me the privilege of preparing this foreword.

FOREWORD

I'm quite certain that Getting Approved will be of great value to you whatever your credit standing may be. In this day and age, when credit dominates almost every aspect of our personal financial growth, this book is a powerful, indispensable tool.

Benjamin DeLeon
Author,
"Entrepreneurship: The SuperCareer
of the 90's"

Preface

Financial institutions and merchants expect consumers to be well-informed on our credit system, yet they provide little if any assistance to guarantee that we are properly educated on how to secure credit and handle the responsibilities that go with it. Banks and thrifts, along with other credit providers are equally guilty of enhancing the mystic character that shrouds our credit system. To a large extent effective, keeping consumers in the dark instills the "importance" of credit, that the struggle we encounter will make us strong and "saint-like" in our credit transactions.

These inadequacies on behalf of the American credit system lords is the celebration behind the success of my earlier works, including my last book, "The World of Credit," which has been purchased by libraries, schools, universities and bookstores throughout the U.S., Canada, Australia and Puerto Rico.

Although "The World of Credit" dwelled more on defining the credit system, "Getting Approved" preocupies itself with making the system work for you. It was my answer to this apparent credit-illiteracy problem that is so greatly affecting American consumers today.

By exploring the "inner workings" of the consumer credit system, this is perhaps the single most important distinction between "Getting Approved" and others, particularly mail-order books that dwell on "tricks of the trade." Consumer credit is a respectable trade, serious of its purpose and function in our economic system. In spite of its failure to educate our consumers, the credit system is real and does not operate with the use of tricks.

In the following pages, you will learn basically two things: what it takes to "get approved" and how to maintain a good credit rating once you have established your credit.

David B. Triemert

Acknowledgments

Many people were involved in the production of this book. A special *"Thank You"* goes out to Ben Deleon, Denise Novo, Rick and Alice Woodbury, Zora High, Darcy Chappell, Rico Alvarez and Billy Smith.

To my parents, Tom and Ellen, brothers Tom and Steve, sisters Cindy and Vickie. May God bless you all for believing in and supporting me in all my endeavors.

To all my friends and creditors, *"Thanks a million"* for the trust and support you've shared with me over the years.

Finally, to Debbie Fruh for the inspiration which gave birth to my writting career years ago.

David B. Triemert

Introduction

This book offers many helpful hints, ideas and strategies to the person who is just beginning to establish credit as well as to the individual who is making a fresh start in their world of credit.

Nearly everything you are about to read in the pages ahead is based upon my own experience in consumer credit.

In my teens I can remember reading numerous books on starting a business and building wealth. The message I read over and over again was "it takes money to make money," I later learned however, that it didn't have to be "my" money.

During my first visit to the local credit bureau, I found that someone with the same name as I, had credit information showing up on my report. Even worse, it stated that I had six credit card accounts that were turned over to a collection agency. Had I been out applying for a loan, the creditor would have taken one look at my application and said "Rejected! . . . NEXT!!"

Being I was already at the credit bureau I figured this would be a good time to have this cleared from my file. Much to my surprise however, the clerk who pulled the report said it would take thirty days to investigate my dispute. My response was "investigate"—"What's to investigate?" "According to your records here, these accounts were opened ten years ago; that means I was granted them at the age of Seven!"

From this point on, the rest is history. The shock treatment experienced at the credit bureau sparked an interest in me, wanting to know every little detail there was to know about credit bureaus and their subscribers on the Consumer level.

Later on as a consultant in the industry, I came to the conclusion that the "need" for my services was much greater that I could ever fulfill out of my business office, so I decided to write a book on consumer credit.

INTRODUCTION

Like most of the books I ever read on the subject, my first three titles each fell short of what I felt the consumer really needed. I wanted to provide my readers with all the "nuts and bolts" that holds this whole thing together. It was then that I decided to share everything I had ever learned about consumer credit and as a result, my fourth book The World of Credit became a great success.

In writting Getting Approved, my objective is to bring The World of Credit into focus in such a way that the reader gets the maximum benefit from the least amount of effort. The bottom line is: fewer pages, clearer instructions and quicker results.

In *Part One* of this book I hope to instill in your value system the actual importance of establishing and maintaining a solid credit profile. You can not even fully function in our society today without a major credit card. It's a shame, but that's the way it is.

Part Two takes you in the front and out the back door of the Consumer Reporting Agencies, most importantly the Credit Reporting Bureau. Here, you'll learn the inner workings of the system used by creditors for the purpose of "granting new credit" as well as for "blackballing" consumers who've run into troubled times financially.

Part Three covers the different types of financial institutions you'll be dealing with, the people who operate them and the obstacles you'll face when trying to establish credit with them.

Part Four discloses everything you'll need to know "and should know" before applying for credit.

It also defines the different consumer loans and lines of credit that you might be applying for in the future.

Finally, in *Part Five* you'll learn the principles and practices of Smart Credit Management, including a host of advance warning signals to watch for, which generally occur before an individual goes belly-up.

INTRODUCTION

In the event that you might need to know the "legals" of consumer credit, the Appendix contains all the laws and agencies to complain to should a creditor ever violate your consumer rights.

For professional credit counseling services on a local level, I've included a complete listing of names, addresses and telephone numbers to the National Foundation of Consumer Credit Counselor's 250 offices in 44 states.

A Glossary has been provided to assist in the definition and better understanding of unfamiliar words and phrases used within the credit industry.

For your convenience, the Index has been enlarged for quick and easy reference to over 200 words and terms.

From A to Z, everything you'll need to get approved and maintain a good credit rating is right here in this book. All that you need to do is read, digest and follow its instructions. I wish you the very best of success in your world of credit.

PART ONE

THE IMPORTANCE OF CREDIT

Have you tried to rent a decent car lately or check into a quality hotel without having to present a *"major credit card"*? How many merchants do you know of that will accept a personal check without a major credit card as a second form of identification?

Times have changed. It's no longer possible for the average person to purchase a new automobile using "all-cash." How anyone could buy a modest home nowadays using "all-cash" is unheard of. Your grandfather's advice to "pay cash for everything" is still a great principle to live by, however, most people are unable to practice this value because of the major economic changes that have developed over the years. Our "cash society" is quickly becoming what's known as a "credit society."

Although "cash" still has a voice in todays economy and will continue to for some years to come, credit has become "king" for many consumers and the numbers are increasing. More and more individuals are being forced to involve the use of credit in their purchases of major necessities such as homes, automobiles, and college educations.

On the flip side of the economical reasons behind our growing "credit society," there's a few more factors to address which in essence forces us to develop and use credit.

"In order to be a fully functioning consumer in todays day and age one must be a member of the society who carries at least one major credit card; be it Visa, Mastercard, or American Express."

It used to be that a person could rent a nice car or check into a decent hotel with "cash" but things have changed. Today Hertz Rent-a-Car and Hyatt Hotels want a major credit card. And they have good reason.

Many merchants have come to realize that anyone who has at least one major credit card is not a total deadbeat, anyway. This person renting the car or hotel room must be somewhat responsible if they have a Visa or Mastercard. Any flake can carry a few hundred dollars cash in his pocket. Think about it. If you were Hertz, would you trust a $15,000.00 automobile to a person who didn't show at least a minimum amount of responsibility? What if he gives you a $100.00 cash deposit to rent one of your cars for the weekend and it comes back in shambles? What if it comes back with dents and scratches and cigarette burns in the seats? This actually happens.

How about the hotel owner? He provides a nice clean room for you to sleep in and after you check out, the maid's heart skips a beat when she opens the door to clean your room. The beds are torn up, the mirror is broken and all the bath towels are missing. Upon further investigation, it's found that there's an unpaid bar and restaurant tab at the front desk, $40.00 worth of long-distance phone calls and two movies that weren't covered with the $70.00 in cash you paid for the room when you checked in the night before. And where are you? Probably on a jet at 35,000 feet or 100 miles down the road, moving on to your next destination. Of course this is an extreme example but you get the picture. Many people have walked out of hotels without paying a restaurant tab or telephone bill.

Why is a major credit card required? Well, the first reason is that you show at least some degree of responsibility and stability. Deadbeats and flakes don't usually get issued credit cards.

Reason number two is that car rental agencies engage in a practice where if you drop the car off with excessive cleaning and maintenance work to be done, they'll wait and fill in the final balance after the car has been refueled and checked over as far as physical appearance is concerned.

The hotel? When you sign that credit card slip, it's like a blank check to them. If you leave without checking out at the front desk, bar and restaurant tabs or any other charges for incidentals will be added to your bill before they send it to the bank for payment.

Each and every day, we move further away from a "cash society" and closer to that of a "credit society."

They (our federal government) may even try to do away with cash altogether in the future. With this, you wouldn't even see your paycheck anymore. It would be deposited into your savings or checking account automatically, and to disburse funds you would either write a check or use a debit card which is linked directly to your savings or checking account. Each purchase is then subject to your having enough money in the bank to cover the cost of the item.

"TWO FORMS OF ID REQUIRED"

How many times have you seen a similar slogan (as above) posted at the check-out stand of your local grocer? They all have it, it's the best way yet to reduce the chances of excepting a forged or stolen check.

Nearly anyone can have a fake identification card made up to match the name of that on a lost or stolen check. They are readily available at your local pool hall or bus depot. But it's much more difficult to obtain a major credit card bearing the same name as it appears on the check. Asking for a second form of identification such as a major credit card is largely used to prevent the crimes committed by bad check passers.

Most banks and thrifts (Savings and Loans) will use the same policy when opening up a new checking or savings account. They already have enough fraud and theft "inside" their organizations; asking for a major credit card as a second form of ID reduces their losses from the "outside." Another reason banks use this policy is that it "forces" consumers to be involved in the credit system, whether the consumer wants to be involved or not. Millions upon millions of dollars are made each year on "annual fees" alone. And most consumers who have credit cards use them. Banks are a major sponsor in this ever-increasing credit society we live in today.

DO I "NEED" GOOD CREDIT?

Any person who desires the convenience of being a fully functioning consumer in a cash-credit society must, of course, maintain a respectable credit profile.

By looking back in recent history and comparing that with where we are today, there's every reason to believe that credit will play an even greater role in our lives in the years to come. It's already reached discriminatory levels in several areas of our lives. Without a major credit card, you no longer shop for the best rate on a rental car, you seek those who rent older, less desirable cars on a large "cash" deposit basis.

With banks requiring this "second form of ID" to open

a checking or savings account, you're stuck with keeping your savings at home and using money orders for paying bills unless there's still a bank in your area that will open new accounts based solely on a drivers license or state ID card.

"Consumers today 'need' to establish and maintain a good credit rating just for the sake of being able to function properly in life with the least form of resistance from lenders and merchants that require the use of a major credit card in your business transactions with them."

IS "CREDIT" GOOD OR BAD?

The use of credit is neither good nor bad. The word itself "credit" is derived from the latin word "credere" which means "belief." "Belief" then is considered a positive, uplifting word in the English language suggesting the word "credit" should then be a positive uplifting experience as it is for millions of consumers.

On the other hand, the misuse or abuse of credit creates negative, costly and counter-productive experiences for those less aware and irresponsible in the proper use of credit.

"Credit in and of itself is neither good nor bad. People with good habits generally do good things with credit whereas people with bad habits generally end up hurting their reputation among the credit industry."

Some individuals will argue that the "use of credit" and the overall "credit reporting system" carries with them, some evil undertones.

Many of the remaining "pay cash only" consumers believe that the credit reporting system will be abused more and more by government and certain individuals in the future for monitoring and/or investigation purposes, creating an invasion of privacy in our lives.

Although there could be some truth behind this, one can still maintain the privileges of carrying a few major credit cards without being a part of the American credit reporting system. This can be achieved by applying for major credit cards from major banks overseas. Most foreign countries who allow credit card issuing on an international basis do not use a social security number system, which happens to be the "heart" of the American credit system. Your social security number is a key element in your credit profile.

Whether your Visa card is drawn on Bank of America or Bank of Switzerland, the merchants don't care. All they're concerned with is that they get reimbursed by the issuing bank, where ever it may be located.

Regardless of the many pro's and con's on the use of credit and the credit reporting system, one thing remains clear and that is the fact that credit is important to have and in many cases, it's a necessity.

Homes, automobiles and educations are very important in our society and yet they are unattainable for most young adults without some form of credit.

Credit could be of more value to you than you may have realized in the past. After all, membership has it's privileges.

PART TWO

CONSUMER REPORTING AGENCIES

Along with our ever-increasing "credit society," scores of consumer reporting agencies have been developed across the nation, the most popular being the Credit Reporting Bureau.

Years ago a merchant or lender would use the telephone to check an applicants credit history by calling his previous creditors for reference, but today for the most part, it's all done by computer.

When you apply for credit, the information stated on the credit application is fed into a computer which is linked up to one or more credit reporting bureaus. This is where your credit file is born. It will list your name, address and previous address, employer and social security number. It also lists who your creditors are, how much you owe them, the manner in which you pay your bills and any previous credit experiences you've had over the last seven to ten years.

It will also show whether you've ever been sued and placed with a judgement or if you've previously filed for protection under one of the federal bankruptcy acts. These bits of information are what makes up your consumer file.

In addition to your consumer file, there may be information stored about you concerning medical histories, records of arrest and things of that nature, but these items do not show up on your consumer file. This information is used for insurance, employment and investigation purposes only. It's known as an "indefinite file," meaning it never gets deleted from your file as is the case with information contained within your consumer file.

"Presently there are some 2,000 credit bureaus across the country. Many of these will be offices of the five major firms." The five major credit bureaus starting with the largest first is TRW. The next largest is Trans Union Credit Information Company (TU). Third in the order is Credit Bureau, Inc. (CBI), fourth is Chiltons Creditmatic System, and fifth is Associated Credit Services, Inc. (ACS), formerly known as the Pinger System.

Recently, TRW acquired Chiltons and it seems as if the two systems will become one; at least in certain parts of the country anyway.

Just to give you an idea as to the size and caliber of these giant information gathering systems, TRW has over 150 million consumer credit reports on file, Trans Union has over 140 million credit reports on file and CBI, Chiltons and ACS combined hold well over 300 million credit reports on file. Combined, they produce over 200 million consumer credit reports annually. Business credit ratings are supplied by either Dun and Bradstreet or by Standard and Poors.

It would be wise to call a few merchants or lenders in your local trade area and simply ask them who they subscribe to for credit reports. Most will give you the same answers. Most will give you at least one name of the five major credit bureaus, if not two or three names.

Once you have the names of the major reporters in

your local trade area, you'll want to get a copy of your credit file from each of them, even if you never had any experience with credit before.

It's not uncommon for the credit bureaus to record derogatory information under your name which does not belong to you. This happens quite often, especially among people who have common last names.

Many times, a man and his son who share the same first name will see their files get crossed with one another. This can cause a lot of problems, especially when Senior is out trying to buy a new car and Junior's "delinquent student loan" comes up on his file. Credit bureaus have proven to be somewhat sloppy in the service they provide.

This negative or incorrect information can be removed from the report but it's very inconvenient and time consuming. And until it's removed or corrected, most merchants will just assume that this is in fact Senior's delinquent loan and, in most instances, the request for new credit will be denied until the matter is resolved.

If credit bureaus were to match up social security numbers and dates of birth, a lot of this inaccurate reporting would be eliminated. The same holds true if they were to use Jr. and Sr. more often as a means of determining who's who.

"Credit bureaus are in the business of collecting information on consumers and selling it to merchants and lenders who want to check your past credit experience. The more information they can record about you the more valuable their service becomes." You'll also find that most credit bureaus are in the bill collecting business, either directly or indirectly.

It's a most vicious circle. The lenders and merchants pound us with some of the slickest advertisements man has ever been exposed to and then the credit bureaus come in and sweep up all the dirt.

In the beginning of this chapter, It was said that regardless of your credit experience to date, find out who the credit bureaus are in your area and get a copy of your report. If they don't have one on you, start one! When you receive your reports, check each detail on them to be sure everything is accurate and up to date. It's strongly recommended that you pull all of your reports regardless of your past experience; it's best to make sure that your reports are correct and up to date now, than to be faced with the possibility of having derogatory remarks come up the next time you apply for credit.

Credit reports cost between $5.00 and $15.00 each. They can be obtained for free if you have been denied credit in the last 30 days. Some state laws allow 45 days. If there are two or three major reporters in your area, the one who supplies your creditor with the report where a denial was based, they must give you the credit report at no charge. With a small membership fee, TRW Credentials gives free credit reports to its members.

Married couples have separate reports. Joint credit will usually reflect on both reports. Some of the husband's sole and separate accounts may even show up on the wife's report. This is most common in the community property states such as California. Non-community property states will generally separate the husband's credit from the wife's unless it is a joint account.

There are two other ways to receive a copy of your report. They are by mail or in person. Getting a copy in person is by far the best way because you can make any necessary changes right there on the spot! To get a copy by mail simply call them first to see what the charge is (providing they didn't supply your report to a lender who turned you down for credit in the last 30 days or so) and then write them a letter giving your full name, Jr., Sr., etc., your maiden name if you are married, your present address, previous address, social security number, date of birth, and a check or money order for the cost of the report. Sign and mail your request. Once you receive "all" of your major credit reports, you now have your "credit profile."

"Note: credit bureau's only gather information supplied to them by creditors. They also use a service who scans public records for bankruptcies, liens and judgements. it's your responsibility to make certain that your credit reports are accurate."

Credit agencies only gather and store information and produce credit reports for their subscribers based on the data they have recorded on you. Furthermore, you should do a "credit check-up" at least once a year just like you would an annual physical and make sure your reports are accurate. Don't leave this up to the credit bureau because they won't do it.

Each credit bureau is separate. TRW, for example, has offices nationwide which are linked together, but they don't exchange information with the other reporters. They keep their information to themselves. Now there are *credit reporting services* that mortgage companies and landlords use. These outfits subscribe to the major credit bureaus and produce what's called a "standard factual credit report" using information obtained from one or more of the credit bureaus. On big money deals like new home loan mortgages, the lender will usually pull reports from two or more major credit bureaus themselves or they will have a credit report service do it for them.

"Credit bureaus themselves do not give credit ratings or make decisions concerning credit application approval." Credit approval is strictly up to each individual lender based partly on the information the credit bureau supplies them with.

Many creditors will report your manner of payment to the credit bureau each month; others will report every three, six or twelve months. Many banks won't report an installment loan until it's been paid in full, at which time they supply the credit bureau with the manner of payment and satisfaction of the loan.

Some smaller merchants and lenders won't report at all. It doesn't pay for them to report. Mortgage companies don't usually report your manner of payment. Oil companies don't usually report either. If your Shell Oil card account is turned over to a collection agency to satisfy payment, then, yes, it will probably show up then as a collection account. Yet there are some collection agencies who don't always report either. Keep in mind that each credit bureau has a different base of customers who subscribe to their services.

Sears, for example, may subscribe to TRW and Trans Union (for credit reports to process applications and to report monthly payment activity on their customers) but not to CBI. Ward's, on the other hand, may subscribe to Trans Union and CBI but not to TRW. Some major credit grantors will report your credit activity to all the major credit bureaus in your area. Each merchant and lender will have their own procedure. You can tell who is reporting to which report simply by examining all your credit reports once you have them.

Pulling copies of your credit reports can be fun, that is, if you have decent credit. After you receive your entire profile, you'll probably see some things on there you forgot all about and you may not find some things you may have expected to be on there. You may also find some things that are either outdated, inaccurate or not even yours on at least one of your reports.

Although the credit reporting system in America has some flaws in it concerning the accuracy of its records, it's still by far the most elaborate system in the world.

We have five major credit bureaus in America producing hundreds of thousands of credit reports daily for banks and merchants of every nature.

Each system incorporates their own fraud deterrent programs to help creditor's reduce the chances of granting credit to the common, everyday credit criminal.

One credit bureau system maintains a listing of social security numbers not yet issued or belonging to someone who is deceased.

Another system helps creditors distinguish residences from mail drops, businesses, hotels and prisons. You'd be amazed to learn the number of people who have received major credit cards in the mail while residing behind bars.

And yet another system alerts creditors to the possibility that a name, address or social security number being used, has previously been used for fraudulent purposes. These are very sophisticated systems and they're being approved upon every day.

REMOVING DEROGATORY CREDIT INFORMATION

In the Appendix you will find a reproduced copy of the Fair Credit Reporting Act Law. All credit bureaus are regulated by the Federal Trade Commission. Also, there may be additional State laws that the credit bureaus must adhere to. To find out if there are any additional laws that pertain to the credit bureaus in your area there are two sources you can contact. The first source is the Attorney General of your State, found under Government Offices in your phone book; or, if you know an attorney, you can ask to see his Code of Civil Procedures book and look under the title of Credit Reporting Agencies. These laws are fairly simple to read and understand.

Although the credit bureaus are supposed to operate within the laws governing them, often times they don't. For example, let's take a look at what a segment of the FCRA laws state.

611. Procedure in case of disputed accuracy:

(a) "If the completeness or accuracy of any item of information contained in the file is disputed by a consumer, and such dispute is directly conveyed to the consumer reporting agency by the consumer, the consumer reporting agency shall within a reasonable period of time re-investigate and record the current status of that information unless it has reasonable grounds to believe that the dispute by the consumer is frivolous or irrelevant. If after such a re-investigation such information is found to be inaccurate or can no longer be verified, the consumer reporting agency shall promptly delete such information. The presence of contradictory information in the consumer's file does not in and of itself constitute reasonable grounds for believing the dispute is frivolous or irrelevant."

Now, as to the "completeness or accuracy" of an item on your report, when it's disputed, the credit bureau must investigate the dispute within a **"reasonable period of time"**. Generally, a reasonable period of time is 10 to 15 business days, however, in California, the law says 30 days is a reasonable period of time (the average investigation takes 48 days). After this time period has lapsed, the credit bureau is supposed to remove the item of dispute if the creditor or source that supplied the credit bureau with that information hasn't responded.

Although it can be difficult and time consuming in

getting the credit bureaus to remove derogatory credit information, that's not to say it can't be done. It just takes some time and effort. These credit bureaus are very large corporations and they have a very heavy work load. The pressure in the investigation department must be great—even worse, **"they don't make a dime on investigating consumer disputes!"**

One would think that these credit bureaus would increase their investigative staff to serve the public better but that doesn't seem to be the case. This would increase the company's payroll but it might just as well increase the credit bureau employees' morale and, in turn, provide you and I with a more efficient and accurate credit reporting service.

Some of you may be asking what is meant by "derogatory credit information." Derogatory means anything that "belittles." A 30-day late payment six years ago is basically a derogatory remark. Any incorrect information is derogatory.

All credit information stays on your report for seven years, and ten years for a bankruptcy, or until the governing statute of limitations expires, whichever is the longer period, excluding "inquiries." Get this: paid tax liens are normally removed after seven years from the date they are "paid in full!" This means you could make full restitution on a six year old tax lien and then it would remain on your report for another seven years; judgements, charge offs and collection accounts are removed after seven years, paid or not. It seems that this system is somewhat counter-productive. With the way these laws have been written, it basically says that you're a fool to pay off anything because it will just start the seven years all over again.

If you have an "unpaid" collection account which is six years old, it will fall off your report in one more year if you don't pay it, but if you do pay it, your report will read

"Paid Collection" for another seven years from the date you pay it, and a "Paid Collection" account or "Judgement Satisfied" doesn't do your report a whole lot of good. It still reflects that you were "once" turned over to a collection agency or "once" sued and placed with a judgement!

What a person could do is to use money orders to pay off a collection account, not providing your name, address or account number, yet keeping the receipts in case they ever came after you; and whether they deposit them or not, you'd be over the moral aspect of owing them money. In all, the account would be paid off and still fall off your credit report seven years from the date reported. This would be much better than paying it off and then get hung with a "paid collection" on your reports.

As the system has it—unpaid tax liens remain on your report until they are satisfied. Once they are paid, they will remain on your report as a "satisfied tax lien" for seven years.

Unpaid collection accounts, suits, judgements, or any other adverse information which, from the date of entry, antedate the report by more than seven years, must be removed.

It's weird! A $50.00 collection account is held against you for seven years, but a "driving while under the influence of alcohol" ticket is only held on your driving record for three—five years. Doesn't this appear to be backwards? Shouldn't your negative credit history be removed after three years while the DUI stays on your driving report for seven years? One $50.00 collection account or even a $500.00 collection account won't kill anyone. But one drunk driver can kill a lot of people; even one death is too many. It seems that the big money people behind these large institutions and the high power people in government are more concerned with "money" and the dumping of black marks onto our credit reports than they are about us killing their loved ones while intoxicated behind the wheel. It just doesn't seem right. It's terrible that we are punished "twice as long" for a non-criminal act than we are for a crime that takes thousands of lives each year on our roads and highways.

The way to remove derogatory credit information from your credit report is to challenge the credit bureaus to investigate and verify any credit entries you don't agree with.

A reason for your dispute might be any of the following:

* **This is not my account—please verify and remove.**
* **This is my ex-husband's or ex-wife's account; please remove from my report.**
* **I don't recall ever being (30-60-90) days late on this account—please investigate and correct.**
* **Your report shows this account went to a collection agency; please show me what it was for and when.**
* **I don't believe this is my judgement; please verify.**
* **This is my son's account, please remove from my report.**
* **This account was paid on time as agreed: why does it show as a negative entry on my report? Please correct.**

Be specific in describing your dispute. Those listed above are just samples.

"When you dispute an entry, the credit bureau is required to investigate the matter in dispute with the source which provided the information. In turn, the source who supplied the information

must go back and look up the account in dispute and then answer the credit bureau with information concerning the account status within a reasonable period of time or else the credit bureau must delete the item from your report." What happens many times is that the supplier of the information won't answer the request to furnish updated information and the negative entry will be corrected. What happens is they're caught in a "legal technicality" and the item must be corrected.

When a merchant receives a request to verify whether or not you were 30 days late on your car payment three years ago, rather than pay someone to see if in fact you were 30 days late on a payment three years ago, the request will end up in the trash many times and go unanswered. In turn, the derogatory remark must be deleted. In some cases a firm will be out of business or under new ownership and will not be able to verify information for the credit bureaus. They are too busy conducting their everyday business activities.

For some creditors, finding information about your account for over a year ago is like looking for a needle in a haystack. If they can't find it or don't look for it, the credit bureau must delete the entry.

Many times, a merchant will report a late payment when in fact it was paid on time. It happens quite often. If you don't dispute it, it remains as shown on your reports. Don't let them mess up your reports. You have to fight back.

Liens, judgements, and bankruptcies are all recorded in public records. Here, the credit bureaus subscribe to a service which scans the public records at the County Court House to record judgements and things of that nature. They, too, make mistakes.

As far as the credit bureau making a claim that your request to investigate is "frivolous," here they have to give you a specific reason why they believe this to be true. The FCRA states: **"The presence of contradictory information in the consumer's file does not in and of itself constitute reasonable grounds for believing the dispute is frivolous or irrelevant."** When you send in your disputes, wait approximately 30 days and then write the credit bureau another letter if you've not received and updated credit report from them. With this letter send a copy of the original dispute and remind them that the items disputed were to be investigated within a "reasonable period" of time and that your credit file should have been updated by now. You'll usually receive a reply within two weeks of sending the reminder. (Remember that each credit bureau is separate and that you must make certain each credit bureau's file on you is correct.)

In each credit report the credit bureaus state something to the effect that in the event the disputed item has not been resolved to your satisfaction after the investigation has been completed, you can add a Statement of Explanation to each entry on each report by supplying them with a written explanation.

The FCRA Law states:

> **611.**
>
> **(b)"If the re-investigation does not resolve the dispute, the consumer may file a brief statement setting forth the nature of the dispute. The consumer reporting agency may limit such statements to not more than one hundred words if it provides the consumer with assistance in writing a clear summary of the dispute. (c) Whenever a statement of a dispute is filed, unless there is reasonable grounds to believe that it is frivolous or irrelevant, the consumer reporting agency shall,**

in any subsequent consumer report containing the information in question, clearly note that it is disputed by the consumer and provide either the consumer's statement or a clear and accurate codification or summary thereof."

Once again, it costs the credit bureaus a lot of money to pay employees to add this information to the computer. What will happen, sometimes, is that the credit bureau will just wash their hands of the situation and delete the entire entry and be done with it altogether rather than add it to your report. It takes some effort and patience to have derogatory credit information removed from reports but it is possible. And there's really no reason at all to hire "anyone" who offers to do it for you.

CREDIT REPAIR CLINICS

The Federal Trade Commission warns consumers to "beware" of any business that claims in its advertisements that it can "erase bad credit" from consumer credit reports. Every day scores of people get burned by credit repair clinics promising to erase bad credit from one's credit reports. The fees charged for this service range anywhere from $50.00 to $2,000.00 and the results achieved by most firms are not even worth the lesser amount.

Many companies will guarantee "results" but there's nothing they can do for you that you can not do for yourself and their guarantee disappears when they do. Some firms also state they will get you a major credit card regardless of your previous credit experiences but they don't tell you that you're required to pledge your savings as collateral to secure the account.

Here, too, you can apply for and most likely be approved on a secured credit card without having to pay an additional fee for this service.

By no means are "all" credit repair clinics bad, because their operators are better informed and more experienced than the averge consumer but it could cost a lot of money and wasted time trying to decipher the good from the bad. You'll be far better off to contact the credit bureaus yourself to correct anything that's derogatory among your credit files.

ADDING CREDIT TO YOUR FILES

Any good credit experience that is not reflected on your credit reports isn't doing much good when you're starting to build credit. In the beginning, you'll want as much positive credit information on your reports as possible. After you've obtained all the credit you desire, then it's no longer important to have your non-reporting accounts report to the credit bureau.

Whenever you negotiate credit terms with a merchant who does not report to a credit bureau, make certain that he'll agree to either send a letter to this effect to each credit bureau, or that they'll give the credit information to the credit bureau when they call or write to verify it.

TRW is really picky about what information they'll add to your report. If a merchant does not subscribe to TRW for credit reporting services, TRW won't report your credit experience with that merchant but they are required by the FTC to update and keep current their files as per their subscribers. Trans Union and CBI, on the other hand, may record your unreported credit information for a small fee upon verification. If you just have one entry added, it's about $8.00 per report. It gets cheaper as the number of entries to be added increases.

Following are some sample letters you can use to have unrecorded credit information added to your report.

Sample Consumer Letter

Credit Bureau, Inc.
2223 Wellington Avenue
Santa Ana, CA. 92701

Dear Sir:

In review of the credit report you hold on me, I've noticed that some of my credit experiences over the years have not been reported to you. I would like them added to my report to reflect my complete credit history. I request that you verify the information with the source(s) given below and have them added to my file. Please tell me if there is a fee for this, which I'm willing to pay.

The credit references I want listed in my file are as follows:

Diamond Jewelers, Inc.
1234 Golden Avenue
Your Town, U.S.A.
Acct. #615893
Opened 1/11/84
Closed 1/11/86
Amount $2,400.00—$100.00 per month
Paid on time as agreed
No present account with them

Jessie James Finance Co.
321 Gimmycash Drive
Any Town, U.S.A.
Acct. #
Opened 5/85
Closed 5/86
Amount $1,000.00 unsecured
Paid as agreed—no present account

Sample Merchant Letter

Trans Union Credit
1400 North Harbor Boulevard
Fullerton, CA 92635

Re: U. Ara Pest
Address
Social Security Number
Acct. #711777

Dear Sir:

At the request of our customer, we are writing to state that a loan in the amount of $10,000.00 was made to Mr. Pest on July 1, 1982 and paid in full, on time as agreed, in 48 monthly installments. Mr. Pest does not have any open accounts with us at this time. He has requested that we supply you with this information so that it will be added to his report. He is willing to pay a fee for this service, whatever it may be.

Thank you.

Sincerely,

Leav Mealone
Grump Thrift and Loan

It would be wise to call your local credit bureau and ask about the cost and procedure of adding unrecorded credit information to your files. Most merchants will be willing to supply the credit bureau with your credit activity, but they are not required by law to do so.

CHECK GUARANTEE COMPANIES

Another member of the Consumer Reporting Agency's family tree is the Check Guarantee Company.

Everyday, merchants turn away customers paying by check when they cannot get approval on the account from a check guarantee company. Most retail merchants and lending institutions subscribe to the services of one of these check guarantee companies.

Banks also subscribe to this service to avoid opening a new checking account for a person who already has a record of writing bum checks in the past. In most cases upon opening a new account, the bank will make a phone call to one of these firms to see if the applicant has any prior record of having an account closed by another institution.

The check guarantee company records the name, address and social security number upon notification of any person who has run into difficulties with being responsible in their checking account activities. The bank will supply the check guarantee company with the name, address and social security number to get approval prior to opening a new account. The "path of access" to this information is that of a name, address and social security number.

Check guarantee companies are then supplied information by the bank on any checks that come back N.S.F. (non-sufficient funds) or that of an account having been closed by them because of misuse of that account. This information is recorded and stored on computer for future use. It usually remains on file for 18 to 36 months, whereas derogatory credit is stored on computer with the credit reporting bureaus for seven years.

When you write a check with a merchant, the cashier will usually punch your account number into her keyboard, which is directly linked to a check guarantee company. Providing there's no record on the computer of your writing bad checks, the check guarantee company will either call the merchant and give verbal approval to accept the check, or if the approval is done automatically by computer, it will provide the merchant with a code. A code "one" would be allright to accept and the check guarantee company would guarantee full payment on the check if it bounced. A code "two" would mean it's a bad risk; the check guarantee company won't stand behind this one. There are many check guarantee companies and each will have its own system, but they operate similarly to the system just described.

By no means is it OK to bounce checks. But sooner or later it seems to happen to everyone who has a checking account. It can happen for many different reasons. It could be an error on your part in bookkeeping, could be the bank's fault. Your paycheck could bounce, causing all the checks you wrote to come marching home. It can happen to anyone. Just remember that any bad check you write can be recorded and stored for future use to haunt you whether it was your fault or not.

It can be very difficult getting a new checking account opened if you've had one closed before. The only alternative is to open an account with a bank who subscribes to a different check verification system other than the one who has a record of your previous account being closed.

APARTMENT RENTAL ASSOCIATIONS

Renters beware: someone's watching you. Scores of Apartment Rental Associations (ARAs) have been established across the nation over the years, and they have been very busy assisting landlords in screening prospective tenants, shafting renters who've messed up in the past, manager placement and even in representing new legislation locally and on a national basis. After all, real estate is the largest tax paying industry in the country and the landlords can have a lot at stake. Someone has to champion the laws that protect the landlords.

One of the ARAs in California uses the services of three different sources in screening prospective tenants for landlords (who are members of this association). The first source is an "eviction service." This firm scans the public records at your county court house for any eviction papers served on you, whether it was for non-payment of rent, causing problems (parties, fighting, etc.) or for making waste of the property such as anything that would decrease its value. A person could have A-1 credit and pay all his bills on time and still owe a previous landlord money without it ever showing up on a credit report.

The next source used by ARAs is your local credit bureau. Here the Association not only sees what their applicants' past credit habits have been, but they can also get a rough idea as to how much the prospective tenant owes and whether or not he may have difficulties in paying rent.

The third source of information the ARAs often use is the services of a check guarantee company. Landlords want to know if you have a habit of writing bad checks or if you have written any that remain blowing in the wind.

With the rising cost of real estate, more and more young adults are unable to purchase so they must rent instead. Landlords in turn depend heavily on the services of the ARAs to screen prospective tenants thoroughly.

PART THREE

FINANCIAL INSTITUTIONS

BANKER MENTALITY

Understanding how your personal loan officer thinks is very important to your success in being approved for loans through him. This person is a master in the art of saying "no." He has to know how to say "no" or he would end up giving the bank away. He gets so good at saying "no" that the word "yes" is erased from his vocabulary and replaced with words like "probably, I suppose, or sure."

The loan officer uses the word "no" to protect his position and the bank's interest. By saying "no" to an unsecured personal loan, he can later bargain for collateral on the loan, or a co-signer to secure the bank's interest better. On a car loan, by saying "no," if the customer persists, the loan officer can ask for a bigger down payment, once again securing the bank's interest in the loan.

"People who are weak in the ABCs of banking (attitude, belief, commitment) are easily brushed off with the loan officer's firm but friendly "no." These people are time wasters to the loan officer. Anytime he can talk you out of a loan by just

saying "no," he probably just turned down a loan request that would end up in default." He may also have more than one reason for denying your loan request and you must read between the lines with him. He's just like a lot of us. He has two reasons why he won't make the loan, just like we have two reasons why we won't do something we don't want to do. This is human behavior.

The first reason he gives you is almost always hogwash. He might say that you haven't been on the job long enough, or lived at the same address long enough; these could be good first reasons to deny the loan (always listen for, and pay attention to his second reason). Regardless of whatever his first reason is, always say, "OK, I can see where you're coming from, Mr. Loan Officer, but what's the 'real reason' why you won't make the loan?" In most instances, he will then tell you the real reason why he won't make the loan. Maybe you're asking for too small (or too large) a loan. Maybe he wants a co-signer or collateral this time around. Also, it's possible that the bank is too short on funds to loan at the time. Many people with good credit and the available funds to debt service a loan have been turned down on their requests. And then the bank tries to make it look as if the consumer is lacking something.

Banks who run into this problem now and then will never tell a customer they're either short of money or out of money because they're supposed to be a bank, and banks are supposed to have money in them, either for loans or for covering withdrawals.

Once while standing in line at a branch office of a very large California bank I overheard the branch manager tell the head teller that they should have ordered more than the usual $25,000.00 they normally get on Fridays.

My first thought, of course, was "$25,000.00 on a Friday?" That's all the cash they have on hand? How do they expect to cash all of the payroll checks of their customers and the cashier checks received on the personal loans that day, and the savings withdrawals, the people who come in to cash a personal check for $100.00 to cover the weekend? And what about the money needed to fill up the automatic teller machines (ATM's) that are used over the weekend while the bank is closed: What about the business customers who order money for making change on a $20.00 bill in the restaurants, stores and gas stations they own?

Another thing that is drilled into a loan officer's mind are the initials CYA, which stands for Cover Your Assets, or in other words, cover your backside. Asking for co-signers, collateral or large down payments are ways to cover himself. The loan officer is more concerned about his job with the bank than he is with the bank's assets, however, if he makes a bunch of loans that go sour, he's out of a job. His job is first priority, and protecting the bank's interests in a loan is his second priority. They work hand in hand, but his major concern is in keeping his job. **"Bankers love security!"**

Don't be intimidated by banks and their loan officers. There's really no reason to have any fear. The image they project is "all this money" and, also "we're not leaving town; we're here to stay." Credibility is a combination of trustworthiness and expertise. That's why you see all the glass and marble and brass and oak fixtures and expensive office furniture. These things are used to impress you and I, but don't be impressed. Beneath all these expensive trimmings in buildings made of glass and marble is "dirt." The same kind of dirt that is called the "floor" over at Ace-Rents-It, your local tool and equipment rental company. In all reality, your bank is really no better than Ace. Your bank rents money to its customers, Ace rents tools and equipment to its customers; the motive for both is profit. **"Don't borrow money from the bank, start 'renting' it from them."** The rent on their money is the interest they charge. Rent your money from the bank; it's much easier than it is to borrow.

Renting money is an attitude. When we use the "rent," rather than "borrow," a whole new dimension to credit opens up. The attitude of renting money makes it much easier for you to get the money you want and need because you are no longer trying to borrow money or, "beg" for a loan. You are now renting it. When you approach it this way, instead of borrowing, you start to shop for price, you don't have to deal with loan officers you never cared for in the first place; you no longer go in on your hands and knees to borrow money. Instead of looking for a bank that will accept and approve your loan proposal, you're now looking to rent money from someone you want to do business with versus finding someone who will do business with you. The end result is that you get more loans approved at better rates of interest in much larger amounts than if you were to borrow. What's the turning point here? You've created "competition!" Anytime you create competition between banks, your value as a customer goes up.

"Banking has never been more competitive than it is today. Where there used to be a gas station on every other busy street corner, there's now either a bank or a convenience store. Many of these convenience stores even have automatic banking centers in them. You don't have to deal with just any bank that will accept you; you can start qualifying banks that you wish to deal with." Competition is where it's at, folks. Create competition between the banks you deal with. Be like Bert Lance, former President Carter's Federal Budget Director. This guy was a "master" in renting money from banks.

Lance's attitude was, "I don't need your dirty, stinkin' money, Mr. Bank President, because I have all these other banks catering to me. I don't need your money."

Many bank presidents have lunch with their competitors. When one bank, not then renting money to Lance, found that his competitors were, they then started prying Lance's fingers open to get a pen in his hand, all the while saying, "How much?," "Sign here." Lance had bankers calling and chasing him with more and more money to rent. This went on for quite some time before the banks found out that he was using his new money to pay off other money he had rented, somewhat like robbing Peter to pay Paul.

Lance ended up renting over 20 million dollars from 41 banks, on over 300 different accounts! His way of creating competition worked very well in this case of renting money. What was the substance of Lance's key to the vault? **"OPTIONS."** Lance had scores of bank's which would rent him money; why would he need another bank's money when he had all these other banks to deal with? **"Who needs your dirty, stinkin' money?"** That's the Bert Lance attitude on renting money!

"Bank loan officers need to know that you have other options available to you. If they think that they're the only game in town you won't go very far with them. Now, if you let them know that they are really just one of hundreds of banks to deal with (actually thousands), you create the perfect atmosphere for a good banking relationship."

Another thing to practice is asking to speak with the bank president versus going in and sitting down at some loan officer's desk. It's not always possible to deal directly with the president but it's surely worth a try. You always want to start at the top in the Chain of Command and work your way down if you must. This way, you can tell the loan officer that Mr. Bank President referred you to him should the president brush you off. You may gain some credibility yourself this way, rather than saying, "Hi, Mr. Loan Officer. My name is John Doe, no one special—just off the street. I'd like five minutes of your time so I can beg for a loan."

Whenever meeting with the bank president or one of his subordinates, you'll always want to use good mental posture. Act like Bert Lance. Never go in expecting to get loan approval on the same day if you don't have a prior banking relationship established already with that particular bank. Once you have done business with them, the rest is easy. You just say how much you want, and sign the contract. If they ask what the money is going to be used for, say, "What would you like to hear that it's for?" That's posture, folks. **"It doesn't matter what it's for just as long as it gets returned when you're through with it; on time, as agreed, of course!"** After all, you did request a "personal" loan didn't you?

Don't walk into a bank you have never been in before and expect to get approved on an unsecured signature loan that same day. Instead, go in to meet with the president and **"pre-qualify"** him for a possible future banking relationship. Tell him who you are and a little bit about yourself. Explain to him how you're very displeased with the poor service you're presently getting down at Care-Less Bank and Trust. Mention the other banks you do business with, also stating how much more convenient his bank would be, providing he could fulfill your expectations. Make certain you say that you would want to become a "**valued customer**" if you did decide to bank with him. He's always looking for "valued customers."

Be sure and mention all of your associates who also bank with Care-Less and how they're dissatisfied with the service they receive for "all that money" they run through their accounts. Ask if "he would mind" if your associates moved their accounts over to his bank if you decided to do business with him.

Qualify him and his bank and his ability to meet your needs and desires. Don't let him qualify you as they often do. Ask him about his secured and unsecured loan programs. "What's the interest rate, are there any set-up costs involved, what terms are available, what are the 'ceilings' or limits on these loans, who does the approval and how long does it take?" Ask what credit bureaus they use, do they offer a credit card, is there an annual fee or grace period, etc.. Remember Bert Lance's attitude on renting money: "I don't really need your stinkin' money, Mr. Bank President, but I'd like to have it waiting for me should I ever find a use for it." Remember, the one who asks all the questions is the one who controls the conversation and the outcome. Qualify him—don't let him have all the mental posture by asking you a million questions.

Never commit to opening an account there on the first day. See how he warms up to you. If he's hot, come back in a day or two and put some money in the bank. If he's a weird banker and his response is cold, move onto another bank who wants to do business like you want to do business. Be sure and tell him that you despise loan approvals and filling out a bunch of paperwork, but, initially, you'll fill his file with all the necessary information and update it twice a year.

When you develop a good banking relationship maintain it, and keep it active. Don't let it die off or fade away. Rent money, just a small amount, even for three to six months, and then pay it off. Do this twice a year to keep it alive.

Invite the person you deal with out to lunch once in a while. Let "him" pick up the tab when you're through dining. After all, he's the hot shot banker; he's the one with "all that money" over there. Actually, loan officers don't make that much money on their job. The ones who are doing well in life are those who have ventures of some sort going on the side. As for "all the money," well, it's not their money. They count other people's money.

After having read this chapter, there should be no reason at all for your being intimidated when walking into a bank. Bankers are people, too. Stop looking at them as High Priests in Holy Temples. They only perform a job like anyone else. They're just another profit-oriented company among the business community. Bankers put their pants on like any other man—feet first. They're no different, they're just people. Some of the younger loan officers get off on having the power to manipulate your success in borrowing money to some extent, but you don't have to buy that anymore. Now you have "options" available to you, and you no longer borrow money. Remember, you rent it! Remember that banks must rent out their money to stay in business. They don't make a dime on deposits alone.

The next time you're in the bank thinking "Why would a big bank like this want to lend poor little ol' me money," put yourself in their shoes and try to get a feel for the pressure in the *loan department* knowing that the banks existence is 90% dependent upon the loan department making new loans.

Renting money is a game. It's a game that involves a winner, far too many times a loser, and a strategy. Make this game be a win/win game. **"Both you and the bank must win in order to continue your relationship."** Since he'll always want to see all the cards in your hand, you might just as well see all the cards in his hand so you can play your cards accordingly.

When developing a new banking relationship, remember that he's on trial, not you. You qualify him and his bank. It's OK to bend a little in the initial stage, but take more and more control of the situation each time you rent from him. Let him know that you're a player, you play the game of renting money. You know all the rules that govern it and you live by them. Don't ever leave a banker hanging out to dry when you rent from him.

Be somewhat patient when you start building your banking relationships. Bankers are not entrepreneurs and for the most part they never will be. Many will remain out in the weeds for as long as there are banks to be bankers at.

"Build more than one good banking relationship. If you're an entrepreneur, build several to start with and always continue to expand your banking relationships. Continue to create more and more 'options.'"

The reason you want to always seek to establish new banking relationships is that even though you get a good rapport going with someone and pay all your loans back on time, you might walk in one day to rent some money and your personal loan officer or bank president may not be there. He could get transferred, fired, or just sick and fed up with that bank's management and quit. Sure, you have good credit with that bank to show the man replacing the guy you knew, but it's not the same. You'll have to educate this guy on how you're used to doing business, just as you had to do with the first guy. That's why you want to maintain more than one good banking relationship and continue to establish new ones. Another reason to seek new banks to deal with, is that you might pull up one day, all fired up, and ready to rent some money, only to find that the bank is closed, yes, closed, insolvent, bankrupt! This usually takes place on Fridays though.

With banks dropping like flies, there's a chance that the next one could be yours. Where do you stand then if this was the only bank you had established a relationship with?

It doesn't matter how big your bank is and how solid you may think it is. It's a shake-out period for banks. Look at the size of Continental Illinois. How about Seattle First National? Continental was bailed out by the government but, what do you suppose happened to all those loan officers?

BEING SELF-EMPLOYED

Keep in mind these initials, J.O.B. The J.O.B. stands for Jumping Over the Bumps of being self-employed while applying for credit. The J.O.B. also spells "Job" which is the answer to many problems that stand between you applying for credit versus being approved when you're self-employed.

There are all kinds of tactics people use to overcome these high hurdles of getting credit when self-employed. Some people will hire an accountant to create bogus financial statements to substantiate the proper "income to debt ratio" and "net worth" in order to get loan approval but that's not right.

What's recommended is that you get a job. Don't go out and apply for a new job to replace your business or to have a secondary income. Become an EMPLOYEE of your business instead of saying you're the "owner" of your own business.

"You need to be 'normal' when applying for credit. Banks and merchants are not all that crazy about doing business with self-employed people, especially when the business hasn't much of a track record to base profitability and stability on. Creditors would rather do business with the normal everyday man or woman because of the lower risk factor."

Banks don't really want to do business with hot shot real estate investors or "set-the-world-on-fire" entrepreneurs. They will do business with these people, but they would prefer doing business with the average person.

The perfect scenario of a good credit risk is a person who has a nine to five job and has been on that job over five years. Let's call him John Normal Jones. John has lived in the home he's buying for 3 to 5 years. He drives a small to mid-size car that is being paid for on time, as agreed, in monthly payments. John is married, his wife works part time outside the home, and they have a few children. John has a savings account, checking account, an IRA, life insurance, some municipal bonds, and a healthy credit profile. John gets up everyday and goes to work, puts in his eight hours, five days a week, collects his paycheck on Friday and deposits it in his checking account and pays his bills before the due date.

John is ultra conservative. He never rocks the boat or makes any waves. He's almost like a robot whose actions are automatic. Creditors love John because he is the perfect model of a good credit risk.

However, Don, John's neighbor, is a whole different story. Don is one of these high-risk entrepreneurs the banks are not fond of doing business with. The creditor never knows when to expect payment from Don. He has his own business and is very proud of it. He'll burn the candle at both ends and sometimes in the middle. Don rocks the boat and makes plenty of waves. He's convinced he's going somewhere in life and he understands in advance that there will be bumps to jump over, mountains to move and plenty of risks to take. Don's the high spirited fellow you see in the bank talking to the loan officer. Don looks like he owns the bank. He acts like he owns the bank, and although he may not have any stock in the bank, he very well could be one who controls it.

A really good "Don" can control the bank without

having any of his own money in it, simply by being the one who owes the bank the most money. Believe it or not, it's actually better for Don to owe the bank $5,000,000.00 rather than $5,000.00 because the bank will have a vested interest in Don's success.

Now if Don needs $1,000,000.00 to cure a problem, or to invest in a venture that will pay back the $5,000,000.00 he owes them, Don has a much better chance at getting this loan because the bank can't afford to let Don fail on paying back the $5,000,000.00 he owes them. Don is a big thinker and a big doer. He knows how to play the game and it sometimes scares the bank to have someone who's mastered the art of credit when you (the bank) are the author of it. Banks are sometimes fearful of Don because there have been other "Dons" who have robbed the bank without a gun.

Don's a high flyer; he can go through life by the seat of his pants. He's the kind of guy who can lose $10,000.00 in a day on a business transaction without blinkin' and eye. Don just keeps on keepin' on. He has a dream, a goal, a vision of a better tomorrow; he follows that dream. Many bizarre events can happen along the way, but nothing can stop a determined Don outside of death itself! Even with death, a "well-seasoned" Don will have his funeral financed!

Is there any question why banks are very cautious in dealing with a "Don?" Being self-employed is the "pits" when applying for credit if you come on as the owner of your own business.

Self-employed people (let's call them entrepreneurs) are usually required to produce their last three years' profit and loss statements, income tax returns, and a balance sheet or "financial statements." Presenting yourself as an entrepreneur to a loan officer can be a real challenge in getting a loan approved. That's why you want to get a J.O.B. Become an employee of your company if you have a hard time getting credit. Don't list yourself as the owner or president; let your wife be the owner and president and you be the vice president of sales, or marketing director, sales manager or janitor, but don't be the owner or president. Become an employee of your company. Make sure that whoever answers your phone is equipped with these four pieces of information about you when you're applying for credit:

1. Position or title
2. Monthly/yearly income
3. Years on the job
4. Supervisor's name.

Have this information handy for lenders, verifying your income and length of employment. Pay yourself a salary and become an actual employee of the company.

If you prefer to remain calling yourself the owner or president of Fly By Night Enterprises, then you should get all your ducks in a row when applying for new credit.

The key to jumping over the bumps in applying for credit is to get a job. If you insist on telling your future creditors that you're the president or owner, then start a file on yourself to give to creditors when you apply for credit. Note: The fatter the file, the more money you can borrow. The loan officer will request a profit and loss statement, tax returns and balance sheets from the last three years. Give it to him! Throw a bunch of other goodies in with it. Put your credit reports in there, a copy of your high school diploma, a picture of your family, a computer run of your checking account, your college degree or certificate—fill that baby up! He won't read it all—99 times out of 100, he won't go through all that stuff.

Why the big file? Well, that's his "out" if you default on the loan he just made you.

In the event he's ever called into the Board Room on

behalf of the bad loan he made you, that file is his trump card. He's going to dump that puppy out on the table in front of his superiors and say: "Look at all the information this person submitted; he's the last person I ever thought would default on a loan. Look; here are his financial statements, tax returns, checking and savings account activity sheets, his high school diploma, college degree, and even of picture of his family. Mr. President, this is the last person I ever thought would default on a loan."

The bigger the file, the fatter the loan. Playing the game. That's how the big shots do it and you can duplicate the process.

If you're self-employed, either get a job or start building a file like the one mentioned with all the goodies in it.

WOMEN AND CREDIT

Many women complain about not having any credit; most of these are divorced or never married. A lot of married women don't even realize they don't have credit, but they'll figure it out if they get divorced or if something happens to their husband—God forbid! The reason behind this is that men are often the ones who have the credit in the marriage. The woman assumes she has credit, providing her husband signs for all the credit. Until he's no longer there to sign for their credit needs, the woman often believes that she has credit, too. Unless it's being recorded on her credit reports (if she even has a credit report) she won't have any credit in her own name. When he's gone, so is his credit, and she finds herself as a middle aged woman who has no credit. This is a very large problem among women today.

One of the biggest causes for all these women having no credit is because of divorce. Either she didn't have any of her own credit while in the marriage, or the credit she shared with her husband took a turn for the worse as a result of the divorce. Many times, in divorce, a resentful husband or a rebellious wife, or vice versa, will use the credit cards to charge up the world in an attempt to get the better end of the divorce, or to get back at their spouse. Whatever the case, both reasons contribute to the detriment of credit.

"The key to your credit success, regardless of your marital success, is that you must build your own 'sole and separate' credit. You need to build and maintain credit in your name alone."

There are a lot of benefits to be gained from building sole and separate credit. First of all, in the event the marriage doesn't work out, each spouse may part with their own credit. If the wife was always on time in paying her bills, she will have good credit when the marriage is dissolved, whereas if the husband was habitually a poor credit risk, she doesn't have to pay for his neglect or irresponsibility.

Another good reason to have separate credit is in the event a financial tragedy comes your way, leaving you with no alternative but to file a bankruptcy. Providing it's feasible, one of you could file bankruptcy while the other maintains good credit in the marriage. If you're both in the same boat and it's sinking, you're sunk. Having two boats with one going down, there's still one afloat which you can share until you get another boat.

If your husband has all the credit now, have him put you on his accounts as a "**sharer**" of the account. You want to be sure you only "share" the privileges but not the **"contractual liability"**. If he messes up in the future on the account, you don't go down with him on it. It may show up negative on your reports, but you can dispute it saying you only "shared" the account, but not the responsibility of paying it back. If the account remains in good standing, then you can use the account as a reference, saying you share this account with your husband. Make sure it reflects on your credit reports as being positive; if it's negative, get it off of there.

Some men don't have credit, but their wives do. You can apply this same principle. Put your name on your wife's account as a "sharer" of this account.

If neither the wife nor husband has any credit, then both sign on the account as **"joint"** in privileges and contractual liability. Do this until you both have enough credit built up to get credit singularly. Then, as your new sole and separate accounts begin to get established, start closing the joint accounts you first shared. The end result is that you both want your own credit to be "sole and separate."

As for who to pay late when it's called for after you both have separate credit, the answer is very simple. If you're the husband, you're saying pay late on her accounts. But if you're the wife, you're probably saying let's pay late on his accounts. You'll have to work this out between the two of you.

If the wife is not working, she can still get credit reported on her reports by being a sharer of the account. If divorce comes along, she might then start working for a source of income to support herself, and she would have some good "shared" credit on her reports to use as a reference on her applications for new credit in her own name. This is provided he maintains good credit after the divorce. If he quits paying his bills right after the divorce, it will most likely come up negative on her reports, but she can remove it by saying she didn't share the "contractual liability" on that account. Providing you didn't sign the application for that account, there is really no way they can leave negative information on your report. Ask them to produce an application for credit on that account that bears your signature. They can't do it providing you didn't sign it to begin with. How can they hold you liable for something you didn't authorize? Share the good and dispute the bad.

The way to become a sharer on an account is to have the account holder contact the lender or merchant in writing and request that this other person (you) be added to the account. Include the sharer's name, address and social security number.

In the following chapters you'll learn how to build credit, if you don't have any now. In the Appendix is a reproduction of the Equal Credit Opportunity Act. This will tell you what your credit rights are as a woman, while applying for credit.

Joint checking accounts can be good or bad. It's easier to make deposits in and keep records of one account than it is for two. If your husband is careless and causing problems with your checking account, then set up an account under your name alone. A clean checking history is very helpful in building credit. We'll talk more about this later.

CHOOSING A BANK THAT'S RIGHT FOR YOU

In choosing a bank that's right for you, keep in mind that the two main objectives are: finding a bank that is aggressively seeking new business, and making sure you can develop a personal banking relationship with them. Don't just walk into a bank and open up an account. Be fussy about who you bank with. Spotting an aggressive bank to deal with is fairly easy. Just watch for those who are doing a lot of advertising.

The cost of advertising can get pretty expensive. In order to profit from it, banks need to pull in new customers for loans and lines of credit. It would be foolish to advertise if they didn't have an abundant supply of money to rent. Another good sign is when you see all these credit applications on top of cigarette machines in hotels, restaurants, and the like. These are the "Credit Card Pushers." They are very aggressive in seeking new business. Ask friends where they know of aggressive lenders—who's easy and who's not.

Merchants who offer credit terms on their merchandise are a good source for finding aggressive lending institutions, especially car dealers. Any good sales manager knows who's aggressive and who's not. A really good sales manager can put almost anyone in a new car.

The best banks to deal with are the "Lone Ranger" banks. They have only one or two offices, not a thousand branches. They are generally more aggressive, more lenient on qualifications, and much friendlier and more personalized in the service they offer. These little one-office operations are sweet to deal with. They have to be more flexible because all the big banks create so much competition for the little guy.

With the small, independent bank, you get service with a smile, and you're often called by name. The tellers remember you enough not to have to see your identification every time you want to cash a check drawn on your own personal account. Small banks don't have a large loan committee that really does no more than shuffle paper. **"They want to stall you for a day or two, just so they don't look "anxious" to give you a loan."**

Big banks have forgotten that the customer is always "number one." They want to act like they're doing you a favor when, in fact, you're doing them a favor because without the customer, there can be no bank.

Large banks can be very impersonal. Nobody really knows you; in fact, they probably don't care to know you. All they want is your money and, occasionally, they'll give you a loan providing you fit into their lending policies. Large lending institutions have a lot of employee transfers and turnovers too. You never know who you'll be turned over to as far as loan officers or personal bankers are concerned. It can change quite often.

Deal with smaller banks. Most of these big guys couldn't care less about you on an individual basis unless you're already a proven High Roller. Then the banks start calling and chasing you with money to rent.

CREDIT UNIONS

Don't underestimate all the benefits one can gain in becoming a credit union member. They are often the best source in town for establishing valuable banking relationships. They seem to treat you like family—it's a family affair. They seem to have a genuine interest in helping you with your financial needs and desires.

You may get a kick out of these expensive TV commercials where some old gold prospector comes out of the hills and into town with his find. He gets approached by several bankers who try to reel him into their banks. He ends up going to the one at the end of town, and here's this old fashioned, honest looking, about-to-retire banker who weighs the precious metal and says, "That's what it's worth, and that's what I'll pay you for it." What they are trying to do with all these advertising dollars, is to project an image of something they are not. They'd like to be old fashioned but all these computers and electronic banking aids have polluted their real purpose in business. Instead of being on a first name basis with a bank or S&L, you're just another number to them. They've moved out of the people business and into a computer state of mind. They don't even think for themselves anymore; it's all done by computer.

One large bank has recently come out with an advertisement that is way off base. They speak very highly of **"service"** but judging by their branch offices they haven't got the faintest idea what service is.

They spend millions upon millions of dollars on advertising. Everyone knows that the message they try to relay to the general public is a crock. Why don't these banks take some of those advertising dollars and use it to put some tellers behind the counter so they can live up to providing the service they speak of? Why don't they use that money to pay some people as tellers to serve their customers properly. They spend their money in all the wrong places, such as expensive TV and radio advertising.

Who do you think is the one who's really paying for all this advertising? Well, if you spend more than five minutes in line waiting to be served, then you're paying for that expensive advertising with the "rotten to the core" service you receive. If every teller window is open and there's a ten minute wait, then it's understandable. But if there are 15 teller windows and only three or four tellers working, and there's a line of people forming a Z-line in the bank lobby all the way to the front door, then you had better deal with someone who really does want to serve you. If these banks continue to operate this way, it will eventually become faster to get a heart transplant than to get a check cashed!

Some of these banks have been around longer than dirt, and still they spend millions of dollars on advertising that could be much better spent in other areas of their business. They continually search for a new "Band Aid" when they're really in dire need of a "tourniquet." They need to start serving people again.

In California it's very rare that a bank has a drive-up teller. There's thousands of housewives who would rather use a drive-up teller than to have to drag their children into the bank only to stand in line with them for 20 minutes. A lot of banks used to have drive-up facilities but they've closed them, probably to save a few bucks on the cost of maintaining the equipment. They don't serve people like their advertisements claim they do.

In California, most banking hours are from 10 am to 3 pm. On Fridays though, some stay open until 6 pm. There's only a few banks who are open on Saturdays; they are still service oriented to some degree. They even have drive up tellers.

It's a wonder how anyone can operate a business on only five hours a day, and still remain in business; how do they do it? **"They set their business hours according to their own desires without giving any consideration to what we, as customers, might want or need."** From here, the rest is quite simple. They jam us into the lobby like sardines and make us wait in line for 20 minutes to let us give them our money. With our money in hand, they pay us a whoppin' 5% interest and turn around only to charge us 18% interest on a personal loan or credit card.

Perhaps what they need is for the public to recognize one day a year as a National Holiday where we all go in and take our money out; call it "Bust the Bank Day." It might help serve as a little reminder that the "customer" is the one who keeps the bank in business. They all tend to overlook this.

Find a credit union to deal with. They, for the most part, still want to fill a respectable and valuable service, and they will go out of their way to achieve such a task. Most will at least stay open until 5 pm.

Credit unions have Visa cards, too, at much better rates than the banks. They have good rates on everything. Often times, their rates are under market on all the different credit lines they offer. Some will even do home loans.

FINANCE COMPANIES

Finance companies should always be considered as a last resort for renting money. First of all, they have very high interest rates, and it's not a "super plus" on your credit reports even if you pay on time as agreed, because it tells other, more conservative lenders like banks, S&Ls, and credit unions that you had to lower yourself to the point of dealing with a high risk, high interest rate finance company.

If you're new to the world of credit, or making a fresh start with credit, then it may be necessary to deal with one of these outfits only to get started. Having a couple of satisfied accounts with a finance company on your credit profile is better than no credit history at all, but it's best to find a credit union or bank to deal with.

Two of the bigger names in the finance company business are ITT Financial and Household Finance. Both are very aggressive and their interest rates reflect it.

Finance companies do a lot of direct mail advertising. They are the ones who send you a fake check for $5,000.00 with your name on it. They say something to the effect that "this check could be yours by simply filling out the enclosed application and returning it at your earliest convenience."

One nice thing about these aggressive lenders is that, once you do business and complete a loan with them, they usually send you an invitation (pre-approved) to borrow again. Banks should practice that more but they have to take a much more conservative approach. After all, they are bankers, and bankers don't chase people (supposedly) to put a new loan in the hands of just anyone.

Finance companies are good to have in your hip pocket for emergency cash. They make personal loans just like anyone else in the business but at higher rates. Some firms advertise "Loans by Mail," or "Borrow $25,000.00 Overnight On Your Signature." Watch out for these ads. They may bait the hook and then reel you in. It's called "bait and switch" or "strings attached." What they will do is grab your attention on an ad similar to this and then try to get you to use your home as collateral. **"What they are doing in essence, is bringing you in on a "signature loan" which actually ends up being a second or third mortgage on your home."** Watch out for these guys; they can be pretty creative.

Many merchants who say "We Finance," don't actually finance in-house. What they usually have is an agreement with a finance company to carry the paper (contract) on merchandise they sell with credit terms. The merchant usually has a good rapport going with the finance company agent. Many times he can boost the agent over the fence to finance a marginal loan request.

Car dealerships who advertise, "We Carry Our Own Contracts" are just as aggressive as the finance companies. They buy their cars wholesale at auction.

Let's say they buy a car for $800.00 and sell it two weeks later for $1,500.00. They'll advertise something on the order of "No Credit Needed" or "Bad Credit OK." They'll always try and recapture their investment in the form of a down payment by the customer. On this example, they would ask for $800.00 down and, perhaps $100.00 to $150.00 per month. If the customer pays as agreed, fine. But if they don't get paid as agreed, they are "quick" to repossess the car and keep the down payment, the rest is gravy. These guys can be some pretty slippery dudes. Watch what you get yourself into.

Finance companies of any sort are a great source for special situations, but avoid dealing with them whenever possible. A bank loan successfully paid in full will look much better than a similar account with a finance company.

LOAN BROKERS

Here's a source which can be very helpful to anyone wishing to obtain a real estate or business loan of some sort. Loan brokers can provide a very meaningful service to you. **"Any loan broker who plans on staying in business must know who the aggressive lenders in town are and what types of loans they make."**

Lenders love doing business with loan brokers. First of all, loan brokers save the lenders from having to do a lot of paperwork. Loan brokers will have the borrower complete all the necessary paperwork in the loan package prior to submitting it for approval to the lender. Suppose the lender approves the loan, they then pay the loan broker a small percentage of the loan as a loan fee, also known as points. A point is a percentile. Two points is two percent and so on. Loan fees or points to the broker will usually range from one to ten points. The lender usually pays the broker but, in all reality, you are the one paying the points through the lender.

"One thing you really want to be aware of is the broker who asks for a loan fee or application fee up front, before the loan package is even submitted or approved." There's big business in selling loan applications to applicants who pay from $25.00 to $250.00 as an up-front application fee. When you pay an up-front fee, who knows if your loan package was ever sent out for approval? It may have gone into the trash without ever being sent out or called into any lenders.

Don't pay any up-front application fees. That would be like paying a realtor a commission to sell your home before it's even listed for sale in the multiple listing book. You need to be aware of these rip-off artists who do nothing more than cash your check.

Never pay a pre-application fee. If the broker really feels he can find a lender to make the loan you request, then by no means should he ask for an up-front fee. He'll get paid for his service after he's done his homework and gets your loan approved.

Loan brokers are a dime a dozen. Don't just let the fact that there is no up-front fee steer you in that firm's direction. Qualify the brokers as you call around searching for the right one. Ask them who's aggressive in making your type of loan. Ask them how busy they are. If they've been sitting around staring at the walls while the loan brokerage industry is booming, then either they're not aggressive and hard working, or they're not established yet. They may have just opened their business last week for all you know. It doesn't require very much at all to get in this business and call yourself a loan broker.

Some loans, such as real estate mortgages, will require a broker to be licensed by the State to broker such loans. Be cautious in whom you do business with. Even if they don't charge an up-front fee, you still don't want them pulling your credit reports unless they are established and aggressive. You don't need any unnecessary inquiries added to you credit reports.

A good loan broker can be worth his weight in gold. He knows what the lenders expect in a loan package and which lender is best for each type of loan. Lenders would much rather deal with a loan broker than the borrower himself because a good loan broker knows the business well, and also, he speaks the language.

PART FOUR

APPLYING FOR CREDIT

Here are the actual steps you'll want to take in putting your best foot forward when applying for credit. For those of you who are already established, keep reading, you'll find some more bases to cover when filling out your next credit application.

The first step in applying for credit is to make sure your credit reports are in their proper form. There's no sense in applying if there is still derogatory information on your reports. Be sure everything is up to date and accurate.

Next, a checking and savings account are vital in applying for credit. At least one of each is necessary but two would be even better. Savings accounts should have some money in them—at least $100.00. You'll also want to make deposits and withdrawals from time to time just to keep them active. Otherwise the accounts get turned over to your State Government after a period of time and become a part of the "$25 Billion" kitty that they aren't real concerned with finding the rightful owners of.

Checking accounts must remain active but, most importantly, they must be free of any bounced checks. Creditors are looking for stability and responsibility here. They want to see how you handle your checking privileges. If you have a history of writing bad checks, chances are very good that you won't handle your charge card payments with tender loving care either.

There are several different types of credit you may apply for. Let's take a look at a few of them, and then continue with going over the proper steps to take in applying for credit.

The most common types of consumer credit are:

- **Installment Loans**
- **Signature Loans**
- **Revolving Charge Accounts**
- **Closed End Charge Accounts**
- **Open End Revolving Accounts**
- **Line of Credit**
- **Overdraft Protection**
- **Consolidation Loans**
- **Mortgage Loans**
- **Home Improvement Loans**
- **Hard Money Loans**
- **Home Equity Credit Lines**
- **SBA Loans**
- **Auto Loans**

INSTALLMENT LOANS, in brief, are described as a loan in which the total principal and interest amount is divided into equal monthly payments in spreads of 12 months, 24 months, 36 months, etc. Most auto loans and personal loans are written on an installment basis.

SIGNATURE LOANS should only require one signature. They are not based on collateral or co-signers. They are based upon your character of having rented money in the past and paid it back on time. These loans can be a 30 day note, up to a one year note. You may be required to pay the interest each month and then the principal amount when it finally comes due. The more sophisticated borrower will generally ask that the principal and interest be paid at the end of the term, and then when it comes "due," he'll "roll it over" for another six months or so.

REVOLVING CHARGE means a balance on an account can be paid in full or in monthly payments. Providing you're not over your credit limit, additional charges can be made on this account and added to your next month's billing. The most common charge cards are Sears, Wards, and J. C. Penny.

CLOSED END CHARGE accounts are American Express, Diners Club, Carte Blanche, etc. These are charge accounts which must be paid in full each month. Often, these are referred to as Travel and Entertainment cards (T & E cards).

OPEN END REVOLVING accounts are your Visa and Mastercard accounts. These are the best of all. The credit limits on these are based on your ability to make the payments on them. The interest rates are generally high, but there are some low interest rate cards you can apply for. These accounts can also be paid in monthly payments or in full. Fully 75% of the banks issuing these cards still have a grace period. These are the hardest cards to obtain at first in building credit.

LINE OF CREDIT is most commonly used by businesses. These can be reserve lines of credit for meeting taxes, payroll or overhead expenses. They are designed to help see the business man through the lean periods.

LETTERS OF CREDIT are most common among the business community; often they are used in the import/export business. This is simply a letter on the bank's stationery stating that they will guarantee the specified amount as payment to the business or person to which the letter is addressed; this is a service to you as the bank's customer. They do require a good credit profile and the ability to pay them back.

OVERDRAFT PROTECTION is a form of credit which essentially allows you to bounce a certain dollar amount of checks on your account with the bank picking up the tab and billing you in monthly payments—with interest, of course.

CONSOLIDATION LOANS. The purpose of this loan is for paying off your higher interest rate accounts using a lower interest rate consolidation loan. You end up making one large payment each month and if it's structured properly the overall savings can be substantial.

MORTGAGE LOAN is also knows as a Contract for Deed or Note secured by Deed of Trust. These have sharp variances about them but they all pertain to the financing of real estate. Mortgage loans come in hundreds of different makes and styles to choose from.

The interest rates will vary with different market conditions and costs of money to the lender. The most popular mortgage is the one which is amortized over 30 years at which time it's paid in full.

Fifteen year mortgages have been coming on the scene lately and offer some very attractive advantages. For another $100.00 per month or so, depending on the amount of the mortgage, you can pay off this loan in 15 years in stead of 30 years and save thousands of dollars.

Mortgage loans come with either fixed or variable rates, depending on which one you chose. Variable rates start out real low but can cause severe problems when payments are raised in the future. This is a big part of the reason that the rate of foreclosures are so high. **"Variable rate loans are designed to help the 'unqualified' qualify."** Fixed rate mortgages are harder to qualify for but they are easier to maintain when you know exactly what your payment is each month. Each has their own advantages and disadvantages.

HOME IMPROVEMENT LOANS are just that—they are designed for making improvements around the home. These loans are based on the equity in the home and the homeowner's ability to make the payment on this new loan. The interest rates on these are generally higher than the first mortgage rates are. They also range in terms of one to fifteen years.

Check with your local government for low interest rehabilitation loans. They may be able to provide just what you need and can afford if you're in the market for a home improvement loan. They may even have a Block Grant Program if you live in a target area. Also, there are special low interest rate loans designed for the elderly and the handicapped. Contact your local HUD office.

One home improvement loan which only requires good credit (not equity) is the FHA Title One Loan. Contact an aggressive loan broker for more details.

HARD MONEY LOANS or Hard Money Lenders, also known as equity-only lenders or finance companies, are outfits which will often times make a loan when banks won't. Some equity lenders don't even require an income or a good credit history. The loan approval is based on the equity in your home. These people are similar to loan sharks in that they have high interest rates and outrageous loan fees. Finance companies will often make hard money loans, they will also do car loans and personal loans; the rates of interest can be a little steep.

HOME EQUITY CREDIT LINES With the new tax reform laws in effect, interest and finance charges on credit cards will no longer be tax deductible. So, what's been coming on the scene is the Home Equity Credit line because of it's special tax benefits. Basically what you have here is a revolving credit line secured by the equity in your home, which allows you to write off interest on your taxes again. See your banker for more details.

SBA LOANS Small Business Administration loans can be obtained through various banks, and in some cases, directly from the government. These loans are a Federally sponsered, State managed government program set up to assist small business with start-up and expansion capital.

AUTO LOANS They run between 12 and 60 months. The interest rates can be high or low, depending on the lender, and they usually require a 20% down payment and good credit in order to get approved.

All of these types of credit, in most instances, will be approved initially based on scoring enough points on the standard scoring system lenders use. Many facets of your personal life come into play here; they are as follows:

- **Residence**
- **Length of Residence**
- **Lenght of Employment**
- **Type of Employment**
- **Education—Years Completed**
- **Annual Income**
- **Marital Status**
- **Age**
- **Dependents**
- **Credit References**

Look to the next page at the sample point system and see how you add up.

SAMPLE POINT SYSTEM

Residence	
Own	3
Buying	2
Renting	0

Annual Income	
$12,000-$15,000	1
$15,001-$25,000	2
$25,001-$35,000	3
Over $35,000	4

Length of Residence	
0-2 Years	0
3-5 Years	1
6 or More Years	2

Marital Status	
Married	2
Single	1

Length of Employment	
Less than 2 Years	0
3 Years	1
4 Years	2
Over 5 Years	3

Age	
18-25	0
26-65	1
Over 65	0

Type of Employment	
Professional	2
Skilled	1
Laborer	0

Dependents	
One	3
Two-Three	2
Four-Five	1
Over Five	0

Education—Years Completed	
Under 12	0
12 Years	1
2-3 Years College	2
4-6 Years College	3
Over 6 Years College	4

Credit References	
Checking	3
Savings	2
Credit Card	3
Bank Loan	2
None	0

Naturally, the idea is to score as many points as possible without being dishonest. Some people will lie on their applications, stretching their assets or holding back from listing all their liabilities, but it's not recommended.

Let's run through the sample point system. Look for areas in which you can improve upon to score more points in the future.

RESIDENCE. Notice how you get more points if you own your home outright than if you are buying. To rent your home, you receive no points at all. The reason behind this is that you're not building any equity and you don't have any roots planted. You can pack up and leave in the middle of the night before the lender has a chance to place a repo order on your new car or furniture. On credit card applications, they don't call to verify whether you own your own or not. It would cost a fortune to do an ownership of title check on each application, but they do have ways of determining with some accuracy whether you are actually a homeowner or not. Banks and finance companies, on the other hand, may call to verify ownership, as well as the condition of the loan.

LENGTH OF RESIDENCE. If you move around a lot, it would be a good idea to get a P.O. Box. Not the kind at the Post Office, but one with a "suite number" with an address. You can get one of these at a check cashing center. If the mailing address for the check cashing center is 321 Main Street and your post box is #10, your mailing address would then be 321 Main Street, Suite 10 (or unit 10). This is a lot better than using a P.O. Box number. This practice also protects your privacy to some extent. Bill collectors can't just drop in on you at home. It's bad enough that they call and harass you over the phone.

EDUCATION LEVEL. Creditors associate continued education with success. They have found that consumers who've attended college are overall a better credit risk. So, the higher your level of education, the more points you receive.

ANNUAL INCOME. The more money you earn, the more points you earn. The higher your income, the more debt you will be able to pay back.

MARITAL STATUS. You get more points being married than with being single. The reason is that they feel you're more responsible when you're married. Especially for men.

AGE. Being 18 to 25 years old doesn't earn you any points. They won't feel that you're fully responsible yet. These are the years most people are likely to neglect their credit privileges. Not that you can't get credit in these years of life, but most people are not established before the age of 25. The productive years for most people are between 26 and 65, but most people over 65 suffer a drastically reduced income, leaving very little to pay bills with after having paid their living expenses. A lot of health problems set in after people retire which also adds to their being a bad risk

DEPENDENTS. Having one dependent is good because it supposedly adds to your being responsible, but any more than one becomes a financial burden in the creditor's eyes. The more mouths you have to feed, the more clothes you must buy. More than one dependent is an added expense which cuts into the money you pay bills with.

CREDIT REFERENCES. It's important that you have had some past credit experience to share with your future creditors. Here's where the importance of having a checking and savings account come into play. You need at least one of each just to score points. You get added points for having a charge card or credit card to list as a reference. The same holds true for a bank loan or a car that's being financed. Some credit applications will also give points based on your zip code.

LENGTH OF EMPLOYMENT. This is important. Do you change jobs every six months? Lenders are looking for stability here. The longer you've been on the same job, the more points you will get.

TYPE OF EMPLOYMENT. Executives receive more points for their profession than does a tradesman or laborer. Obviously, the executive earns more money but they can be fired or layed off just like a tradesman, and yet they receive more points just for being a professional.

These are the main characteristics that creditors are looking at. With being honest, look for ways you can increase your number of points on this scoring system.

Creditors all use a standard point system similar to this. Each may have a different set of numbers assigned to each category but this is a sample of the scoring system they use. Using the numbers as listed, to pass this test you would need a minimum of 20 points. Check your score and see how well you did. Look for ways to increase your number of points in the years to come.

On credit card applications, once you've passed the point system, they then pull your credit reports. If your score is marginal or borderline, clean credit reports will put you over in many cases.

Before applying for any credit, get a copy of all your credit reports and make sure they are accurate and up to date. If you don't have a credit report with anyone of the major credit bureaus in your area, start one. Write to them and ask that a file be started on you. Supply them with all the necessary information.

In the meantime, don't go out and apply for a bunch of credit. You don't want to pile up a bunch of inquiries on your reports. An inquiry is listed on your report every time a creditor pulls your file to do a credit check on you. These remain on your file for one to two years. Don't apply for credit if you keep getting denied. The very reason for your denials may be because a lot of inquiries are showing in your profile.

Any inquiry which is not followed by a new account opened by the creditor making the inquiry tells other creditors that you were probably denied credit for one reason or another. Several inquiries without new accounts being opened, and reflecting on your file, will tell a prospective creditor that everyone is denying you credit. Why should he grant you credit if no one else will? Why should he take a chance on you if no one else has?

To begin building credit you may need a co-signer. This is where a second party, could be anyone you know, signs on the dotted line, stating that he or she will pay off the new credit account if you don't. They become contractually liable on the debt if you, the primary applicant, default on the account.

The person you would want to co-sign your first credit transaction should have good credit, or at least a substantial income—enough to cover his expenses plus this debt. A high income alone may not be acceptable. More times than not, the "co-signer's credit" rating will play the biggest part of it. A co-signer with good credit will prevent a lot of red flags from being raised, more so than a co-signer with just a large income.

Who do you know who has good credit? How about your mom or dad, brother, sister, friend, relative, co-worker, boss, acquaintance, associate, or neighbor? Surely you must have at least one person in your life who believes in you enough to be of help in co-signing your first piece of credit. If you're a total hermit and have absolutely no one to co-sign, there's still hope.

Whoever it is you have in mind as a co-signer, here's one way they can be of help. First see if they will co-sign a credit application with you. This would be your best bet. Don't apply for a department store card or an oil card; suggest that they help you obtain your first unsecured Visa or Mastercard. Just a $500.00 line of credit will suffice. If your co-signer is nervous about this idea, tell him you will cut up the credit card and close the account once you can obtain a credit card on your own to replace it, or let him use the card and make the payments, just as long as it's getting recorded on your reports. Then you can get one on your own.

Another way to get credit card activity in your profile is to have the cosigner add you to his account as a sharer of the account as mentioned earlier. This can be achieved by writing the merchant or lender who the account is with. You don't even need to use the card, you just want the activity to be reported on your credit reports. And once you are on his account, this would be a good time to apply to the same bank for your own credit card, using the account you are sharing as a reference, of course.

Also, you and your co-signer can take the card he helped you obtain and go to one or two department stores who have an "**instant credit program.**" By presenting your Visa or Mastercard and your drivers license, you can get approved on a credit line in about 15 minutes. The co-signer need not even sign with you.

"The reason in getting a co-signer for a Visa or Mastercard over a department store card is because of the power it adds to your report. A Visa or Mastercard which reflects a good rating on your credit report will be the strongest piece of credit you can maintain because, after all, it's the hardest to obtain."

A car loan which has been paid back on time as agreed is a good piece of credit history, but any credit granted on an **"unsecured"** basis is always better. Find someone who has good credit and ask them to let you share some of their accounts until you can get some on your own.

Another source used to build a credit rating is the "passbook savings loan." This method can later be turned into the "round robin" banking procedure.

First of all, the passbook savings loan is one anybody can obtain. You need to have at least $1,000.00 in your savings account to do this. Banks will normally lend you up to 80% of the amount you have in your savings or certificate of deposit or what have you of "like kind." "Like kind" in this example is any asset which is liquid and can be held as security and can be turned into cash without a discount which would cause the lender to lose money if you defaulted on the loan.

Let's say you have $1,500.00 in the bank. You ask the loan officer for $1,000.00 over 12 months, secured by your savings. Now, the principal amount ($1,000.00) and the rent over a one year period of time might be 12% ($120.00) or a total payback of $1,120.00. Your $1,500.00 savings account would have $1,120.00 frozen in it until the loan was paid for but it would still collect the normal 5 ¼% interest. Your monthly payments on the loan would be just under $100.00. You would now have $1,000.00 cash against your savings to use for payments on this loan.

Let's say you put this $1,000.00 into another savings account where it, too, collected interest. That would decrease the cost of this loan even more. Now let's assume you make monthly payments on this new loan, on time as agreed, for six months. Then you go in and say that you want to pay the loan off. When all the smoke settles, here's what you end up with.

First, the $1,500.00 you once had in the account, which secured the loan, is now down to about $1,450.00 and it's no longer frozen; you can have access to it anytime you choose. Second, you have a credit experience recorded on your credit reports of having rented $1,000.00 which was paid back six months earlier than anticipated. Third, you now have the grounds to go into the same bank a few weeks later and say, "Mr. Banker, I'd like to rent $1,000.00 again." He'll say, "Fine, but we'll need to secure it with your savings again."

When he mentions security or collateral, stand up as if you're about to leave and say, "No, this time I would like to do it on my signature alone. We secured the last one, and I paid it back on time as agreed; we don't need to secure this next loan."

You're not asking him for $50,000.00. You're only asking to rent a lousy thousand bucks. If he gives you a hard time, twist his arm. Say, "Hey, six months ago, we discussed this matter and you said you would like to have me as a *new and valued customer*. You said you would be able to meet my desires concerning credit. I don't need that lousy thousand bucks. I'll go pull it out of one of my savings accounts. I do have other banking relationships outside of this one. I don't have to do business with you. You're not the only game in town; I have other sources I can rent money from when I want it. I don't need your stinkin' money." (Make him aware of all your options; remember Bert Lance's attitude on renting money.)

Now hit him with, "Are you going to rent me the $1,000.00 I request on my signature, or shall I go do business with one of my other sources?" Now, don't say a word, because whoever speaks next loses. If you say another word, he'll probably say no. If he speaks first, then he loses the battle and you get your loan. Don't be afraid to lose, and you'll find yourself a winner almost every time. Make him well aware of the fact that your signature is worth well over a lousy thousand bucks!

Renting money is an "attitude." You'll be able to rent all kinds of money when your attitude towards "you" and "it" are of the proper mind. If you have a problem with developing this attitude, then start looking in the mirror every morning when you get up, and say, "Your signature is worth thousands, baby; you're the best money renter there's ever been; you aren't a Small Fry or McNugget, you're the BIG MAC when it comes to renting money, you're The Value Pak." Develop this attitude and the banks you deal with will be yours. Now, an important step here. Pay the guy his money back as agreed in the contract. Don't leave him hanging out to dry. After you do a loan for $1,000.00, raise it to $5,000.00, then to $10,000.00, and so on.

Now, the "round robin" procedure is really nothing more than a duplication of how you got your first passbook savings loan which was later turned into a signature loan the second time around. The only difference is that you do the same process with two or three banks at the same time instead of just one. It will require a little more money to do it with more than one bank but let's run through the process anyway.

With $2,000.00 in bank #1, rent 80% (or $1,600.00) and use that to open a savings account at bank #2. Then rent $1,280.00 from #2 and use the proceeds to open a savings account at bank #3. With $1,280.00 in bank #3, rent $1,000.00 and put that in a savings account and use it to make the payments on these three loans for about three months. Then go into bank #3 and pay it off, using any money you have left over plus the money frozen in #3. Now, use the proceeds to make a payment to banks #1 and #2. When the next payment comes due on #1 and #2, go in and pay off bank #2. Use the proceeds remaining from #2 to make the payments on

#1 as they come due. When the proceeds from bank #2 are gone, go in and pay off bank #1 with the money in its account.

Now go back to bank #3 and get a $1,000.00 signature loan, hit #2 for $1,500.00 on your signature, and #3 for $2,000.00. Pay these off and keep repeating the process. Ask for more each time you rent from them.

The rent you pay to do this procedure is the "cost" of building your credit rating and signature loan sources. You could easily spend $500.00 on rent doing this. Credit cards are easier but this is an added line of "**no questions asked**" banking when it's fully developed.

This method is rather high tech compared to some of the softer, less aggressive methods. There are some slow boats to China in building credit, but they take just as much effort as with using the major league approach; the choice is yours.

If you're really serious about building credit then start turning some of your cash paying purchases into credit term purchases. Are you going to lay out $400.00 on a new set of radial tires for your car? If so, are you going to pay the service station in cash, or are you going to say, "Hey, look. I need to build some credit; I need to eventually get a credit card because I can't even cash a check without one. Tell you what we can do. I'll give you $200.00 down on four new tires and $50.00 a month for five months; you're making an extra $50.00 by helping me build some credit. Have we got a deal?" If he says no, then argue the point that the tires only cost $200.00, and if you never paid him another dime, he really wouldn't be losing much, but if you do pay him as agreed, not only is he getting full retail on the sale, but he's making $50.00 on top of that and, one step further and most important, he'll have you as a customer for as long as he's in business. If he still shakes his head from side to side, get out of there because he's not your man.

CREDIT CARDS

In the beginning stages of building credit, the oil company cards are easiest to obtain. They usually start you off with a minimum limit of $300.00. They'll check your reports before granting you credit but, in most cases, they won't report your manner of payment. Some of the major oil companies who issue credit cards are Texaco, Mobil, Shell, Exxon, etc. These are the easiest cards to obtain when first establishing credit or re-establishing credit.

If you ever filed bankruptcy or let a bill go unpaid with them, chances are that you're still on file only to be blocked from getting over on them a second time. Many of these companies will maintain an indefinite file on any person who already defaulted on an account. Since they don't usually report to the credit bureau, this indefinite list of deadbeats is their main source of protection from getting screwed a second time by the same person.

Department store charge cards are next in line as the least difficult to obtain. The easiest of the department store cards to get would have to be J. C. Penny. Wards would be the next easiest to obtain in regards to major department store cards, then Sears.

Sears is a good department store card to have if you desire their new Discover card. Sears has entered into banking to capture their share of the billions of dollars to be made in these times of high finance. They've already completed several promotions asking some of their 60,0000.00 Sears card holders to apply for the Discover card.

Before applying for credit with a department store, it's often wise to call their credit department and ask what credit bureau they use for obtaining credit reports. Each department store may pull different reports on you. Call in advance to see who they get their reports from, particularly if one or more of your reports are lean on credit information of past success. You'll avoid any unnecessary inquiries on your reports this way.

After you have a couple of department store cards (if you're starting from the bottom, working your way up), you're then ready to apply for a Travel and Entertainment card. Probably the easiest of these T & E cards to obtain is the Diners Club card. The reason behind this is that Diners Club is owned by Citibank who just happens to be one of the most aggressive credit card pushers in the industry. Another good thing about the Diners Club is that people who maintain a good account with them will probably receive a Citibank Visa.

American Express is very aggressive as well but can be harder to obtain than Diners Club. Once you have a T & E card, it's then easier to get a Visa or Mastercard.

Visa and Mastercard, accepted by over three million merchants in over 135 countries are, by far, the most popular credit cards of all.

Over 150 million Americans have Visa and Mastercard among the seven credit cards the average person carries in his or her wallet. There are over 725 million credit cards in circulation in America.

Among all of these credit cards, there are five Premium cards that you should know about. A step up from the American Express Green Card is the American Express Gold Card. The annual fee for this card is $65.00 and offers cash advance features and credit lines. AMEX card members may also apply for the Optima Card, which is their answer to the Visa Mastercard But that's not all. A step up from these cards is the American Express Platinum Card. This one carries a whoppin' $250.00 annual fee and has no credit limit, and the people who carry this card are probably on the IRS's list, too!

Mastercard also has a Gold Card; the annual fee is $55.00 with a credit line of $5,000.00. Two million Americans have at least one of these. Visa's premium card is called the Premier Visa. With annual fees ranging from $30.00 to $50.00, and credit lines of $5,000.00 and up, there is no reason to wonder why two and a half million Americans have at least one of these cards among the many others.

Interest rates on these cards run between 18% and 21%, with the average interest rate being 18.3%. That's highway robbery when compared to the 10.5% Visa and Mastercards coming out of the State of Arkansas. Them Good Ol' Boys are regulated on the rates they can charge, and in some cases, they will accept applications nationally.

Before getting your first Visa or Mastercard, you really can't be too selective on interest rates, but, when you have one to list as a reference, then you can shop around more. There are a lot of card issuers out there who offer rates of 14% to 16% which are much better than the average rate of 18.3% but some of these have limited market areas.

PLASTIC PURSUIT

Why the big push on credit cards?
Money is the answer, the entire motive is for profit, and the name of the game is Plastic Pursuit. The three biggest players in this game are Citicorp, Sears and American Express. The strategy here is to cash in on the huge profits realized between the cost of money to the bank and the rate of interest charged for credit card purchases. Banks love to buy money at 5% or 6% percent and loan it out at 19% or 20%. These are big spreads, leaving the bank with a "pitch black" bottom line.

Citicorp, the nation's largest banking company is, perhaps, the most aggressive credit card pusher of them all. They have the "shorty application," unlike some bank card issuers who want to know your life story.

American Express has targeted the Ivy League students with the Green Card, saying, "Don't leave college without it." They plan to offer nearly all the traditional services of a bank through its Shearson Lehman Brokerage offices to its customers.

Sears' new Discovery card doesn't have a membership fee; this is unlike most other credit cards. It also offers a host of other benefits to be taken advantage of by Discover card holders. Sears has done very well in all the other services they offer, so there is no reason to doubt the success of the Discover card.

Another big reason for the push in credit card lending versus traditional lending practices is because of the federal regulations that restrict interstate banking.

"There's a gap in the law that allows limited consumer banking services on a nationwide basis. The pushers are taking advantage of this loophole to establish multi-million dollar banking networks without the actual bank." What used to be land, concrete, glass and marble has now been replaced with plastic, about two inches by three inches and a thumbnail thick. With all the other financial services being offered along with being a card holder with one of these giants, it's almost possible to carry your bank in your wallet. That's some progress we've made over the years.

"With all this loose credit available, we will probably see some major problems follow in the near future. Mail boxes now being stuffed with preapproved applications for lines of credit may one day be replaced with hate mail from the pushers saying, 'pay up or else!'"

It's not just the banks and other financial institutions making the big push but a lot of retailers have entered into the game of Plastic Pursuit as well. Retailers feel that if a one-time customer can be approved for a charge card, then chances are very likely that they'll come back for more since they have the plastic to purchase with. With the charge card customers, they can also maintain a mailing list of active customers to solicit with sale information, whereas with the cash paying customers, it's hard to get and maintain a current address to send notices of special sales to.

Be careful with all this easy credit. You can get into financial trouble terribly easy. If you're a "set the world on fire" entrepreneur, take on this easy credit at your own risk. It's much easier to get into debt than it is to get out of debt! Bankruptcy filings are already being filed at record rates.

Credit can be great if it's properly used, but, in many cases, it's not. American people use credit cards today to pay for things they don't really want, don't need, and can't afford to start with, only to be paid for in the future.

Entrepreneurs can often find a way to cover their credit card debt but even the wisest entrepreneur runs into problems now and then that are beyond his control.

For you normal everyday consumers, it would be wise to get an oil company card and a couple of department store cards. Then get a Visa and Mastercard. Once you have these, apply for a low interest rate credit card and cut up your high interest Visa and Mastercard and any other credit cards you have and close the accounts. The only cards you really need are one or two low interest rate credit cards. You don't need department store cards. You only need a few department store cards to get a Visa and Mastercard, providing you are building credit without the assistance of a co-signer.

CASH ADVANCE FEATURES

Many of you will be familiar with what cash advance features are. A Visa with a $5,000.00 credit line usually has a $3,000.00 cash advance in which you can draw on the card at most any bank. The major credit cards which have cash advance features are Visa, Mastercard and American Express. If a Visa is drawn on Bank of America, you don't have to go to B of A to exercise your cash advance. If you have 20 Visa's and Mastercards with a $3,000.00 cash advance on each, all of which were issued by different banks, you can walk into any bank that issues these cards and get a cash advance on each, all at the same time. In other words, by showing the bank teller 10 cards with $3,000.00 cash advance on each, you can walk out of that bank in less than 30 minutes with $30,000.00 in cash and cashiers checks.

Do you think you could get a $30,000.00 business loan from your banker in less than 30 minutes with no questions asked? Of course, they charge a small cash advance fee on each card used, but that's the price you pay for the convenience of "no questions asked banking."

On the American Express Gold Card, you get checks that can be written for cash as their form of a cash advance feature.

A good way to access your total line on a credit card is to open a checking account with the issuing bank and have your Visa or Mastercard linked to it for overdraft protection. That way you can use Visa and Mastercard (via overdraft protection) to cover purchases that could not normally be purchased with a credit card, simply by writing a check.

"Don't buy non-productive merchandise at retail prices that will just end up lying around the house or end up in the trash. If you start using these credit cards to buy the luxuries of life like

boats, motorcycles, TVs and stereos, you'll probably end up in trouble financially. Far too many people use these tools, made for bettering their standard of living, as a means of taking a short cut in life and, in essence, buying their lifestyles on a pay-later basis."

Inactivity is not good, either. Your credit reports reflect your highest limit ever achieved on any card. If you have five Visa cards all with a $5,000.00 credit line, but only used one or two of them for up to $1,000.00, then other credit card issuers will see that you're not even using the credit lines you do have, so why should they solicit your business for taking one of their cards which you won't use either? Many people live only to "get all they can," "can all they get" and then "sit on the can." That's not the purpose of money or credit. To have credit lines and not use them in a productive, profitable manner is poor stewardship. To have credit lines and use them to purchase merchandise or services that won't return a profit or save you money is foolish.

Now, the people who issue Visa and Mastercard are not crazy about using their cards to create profit. They want you to be indebted to them, but only to the amount you can afford to pay. They don't want their credit line to be only "one" of the 50 credit cards you have. They'll say that this practice of obtaining a lot of credit cards to produce a profit is simply not right. On the other hand, however, they'll spend millions and millions of dollars on advertising, saying something to the effect of, "Don't leave home without it!" They don't mind sucking every last available dime out of your paycheck, but they don't want you using these credit cards for questionable business ventures or practices. It's just a matter of opinion.

When you first receive a credit card and if you actually want more cards, draw at least the total cash advance amount available, and then use it to pay the card off. This way it will reflect as having been used and paid back on time as agreed. A card with no activity on it will eventually stop other card pushers from giving you their cards, providing you want more cards.

GRACE PERIODS

Grace periods on credit cards are important. About 75% of all card issuers still offer a grace. Each will vary in length of time but the average is 25-days. This means that if you get a new credit card in the mail and, let's say, you charge $500.00 on it, when the statement comes for that billing, paying off the entire $500.00 within the grace period or before the due date will preclude your being charged any interest on the $500.00. Now, if you only paid the minimum monthly payment, interest will be added on the unpaid balance from there on. Some card issuers will attach interest to your charges the day they are made and others will start adding interest at the beginning of the next billing period. It pays to shop around for a credit card once you're established.

THE SILENT BUMP

To bump your limit on a credit card, you simply pay three or four times the amount of your minimum monthly payment. If your credit line is $2,000.00 for instance, and your balance on the account is $1,000.00, your minimum payment, let's say, would be about $50.00. If you pay three times the minimum or $150.00, and you continue to do so for three or four months in a row, your limit will be raised automatically by computer in many cases. Not all banks will do this, but many will. Their computer is programmed to recognize accounts which have been paying more than the minimum amount. If it finds you have the ability to pay more than the minimum payment, then, with many banks, your limit will be raised accordingly. And why not? Why wouldn't they raise your limit if you've demonstrated the ability to pay more than required? They are in the money rental business and they want to rent as much money as possible to anyone who can pay it back.

Looking at it from this point of view, if you can afford to pay three times the minimum payment on the $1,000.00 balance, won't they want to raise your limit to $3,000.00 knowing you can still afford to pay the minimum payment of $150.00 on that amount? Sure they will, but every bank doesn't subscribe to this practice. However, many banks do. This is what's called the "Silent Bump."

If you request them to bump your limit by phone or mail, they usually send you a long, ridiculous application form to increase your limit. On this form, they want to know it all. It can be worse than the original application you filled out. Furthermore, they scrutinize every detail you give them.

After receiving a new card write a letter to the bank thanking them for the account. Also add that you are somewhat embarrassed about the credit limit, being your other credit cards all have a higher limit. They may end up raising your limit just for writing a letter. You can do this on every credit card you receive regardless of the initial limit they start you at.

AVOIDING INQUIRIES

Earlier it was mentioned that there is a way to avoid getting a lot inquiries on your credit reports and still get as many credit cards as you desire. If you apply for say ten cards, you'll end up with ten inquiries on your credit reports. This is not good. Lenders don't like to see a lot of these on your reports, especially if none of the inquirer's gave you a card or opened an account for you.

Some card issuers have a standing policy to automatically deny a credit application for having over five inquiries that didn't follow up with at least one open account. The best way to avoid a lot of inquiries is to get your name in an interconnect system.

PRE-APPROVED CREDIT LINES

Many smaller banks want to be a credit card issuer but, because of limited facilities for credit card processing and such, it's sometimes difficult for the smaller banks to cash in on the credit card boom. What's been developed is an interconnect system. This is where a large bank will process credit card applications and issue the credit cards for the little banks.

For example, let's say that Mini Savings and Loan wants to get in on the Plastic Pursuit. Mini, however, hasn't the facilities or staff to process card applications and or issue cards. Mini then contacts Maxi Bank to hire their services for card processing. Maxi has several others like Mini which they serve. Mini has a credit application drawn up with their name on it. They place these applications in their business community to solicit business on their new credit card, as well as soliciting their present bank customers. Now you come across Mini's credit card application while shopping one day. You fill one out and drop it in the mail. The application goes to Maxi Bank for processing. Maxi then pulls your credit reports and processes your application. Assuming you're approved on the application, Mini is notified and requested to assign you a credit line. Maxi then sends you a credit card, Visa or Mastercard, with the name of Mini Savings and Loan on it. You make your payments directly to Mini; Maxi Bank may be out of the picture now and your account is with Mini Savings and Loan.

Even though Maxi Bank is out of the picture, your credit information is still in their computer. Maxi Bank can then sell your name to all the other institutions like Mini Savings and Loan or even to the other big aggressive banks so that they can solicit your business as well (or they may even send you one of their credit cards, pre-approved)! This is where pre-approved applications come to you in the mail.

Now the way to avoid inquiries is to ask Maxi Bank (once you know who Maxi Bank is) who else they process cards for. Then go to those other small banks they give you the names of and apply for one of their cards. Let's say you apply at Tiny Savings Bank. Tiny will forward the application to Maxi Bank. Being Maxi Bank still has your credit information on file, providing it's somewhat current, Maxi Bank may use that information versus pulling new credit reports on you. This way you avoid another inquiry on your report.

Pre-approved cards are a result of one bank who now has you as a customer, and sells your name to another bank or series of banks so they can have you as a customer, too.

Another source that sells your name is the credit bureau. It just so happens that they can program their computer to print a list of names and addresses of people with clean and healthy credit files. This list is then sold to lending institutions and merchants who want to send you a credit card.

The lender who buys the mailing list will then do one of two things. First, he might send you a normal application to apply for his credit card. If you fill it out, he will pull your credit reports (an inquiry) and decide whether or not to issue you a card. If you're approved, you'll get a card in the mail but if you're denied he will send you a letter stating the reason why.

If you have bad credit or insufficient credit information on your reports or if it has not been on the report long enough, he'll say his denial was based on information received from TRW, TU, CBI, etc. If you are denied credit for another reason, it will be listed as so.

Some other common reasons for denial are collection accounts, judgements, unpaid tax liens, insufficient income, not on the job long enough, unable to verify income, excessive inquiries, etc. If you feel that their reason for denying your application for credit is weak, get on the phone and call them up. Blow a little smoke at them, not a lot, but just enough to let them know that you feel you deserve the card. They might bend a little and give it to you.

Secondly, a lender buying the mailing list might send you a letter which says: "You've been noticed as a good credit risk in your community. We at New York Credit Pushers Bank understand your credit needs and will make ourselves available to meet them. This is the reason we are sending you this letter stating you've been pre-approved for a $5,000.00 credit line."

Credit card pushers hire writers to draft those silly letters to make it sound sweeter than this, but you get the idea. "Just sign on the dotted line and get $5,000.00 credit on your new Visa."

"When filling out credit card applications, be sure to fill in all the blanks, but never list anything in the "other income" section unless you need your other income to qualify for even the minimum credit line. To list other income is only asking for trouble. The reason behind this is that the person scoring these applications is making about $5.00 an hour and like the rest of us, they, to, are lazy by nature. If they see another income, they probably won't even bother to verify it, and if they did verify it with the source, providing it could be verified, they probably wouldn't believe

it anyway. Never list an "other income" unless you must have it to qualify for even the smallest credit line with them, which usually requires $12,000.00 a year income."

If you're just getting started in building credit or if you're starting over, remember that the "hardest" Visa or Mastercard to obtain is your first one. The rest comes fairly easy.

SECURED CREDIT CARD PROGRAMS

There are some short cuts to getting your first Visa or Mastercard. Even with some bad credit showing on your reports, there are still some lenders who will give most anyone a credit card, providing you put a deposit in a savings account with the issuing bank.

One institution to deal with on a secured Visa or Mastercard, is Home Trust Savings in Vermillion, South Dakota. They only require a $380.00 savings deposit and in turn they will issue a card with a $380.00 credit limit. You can increase your credit limit up to $2,500.00 simply by adding the additional increased amount to your savings upon approval. Providing you pay your payments on time as agreed over a 12-month period, Home Trust will then refund your deposit with interest, and you maintain the credit card now on an unsecured basis like any other Visa or Mastercard.

Your local savings and loan may have a similar program. It would be wise to call around and see what the lenders in your community have to offer on the Secured Visa program.

They will be geared more towards helping people obtain a credit card when there is some past credit problem on the report, or no credit at all.

A current list of Secured Visa and Mastercard issuers can be obtained from Bankcard Holders of America.

Their address is *Bank Holders of America, 460 Spring Park Place, Suite 1000, Herndon, VA. 22070.* BHA also produces a list of low interest-rates credit card issuers. Write for more details.

Another source for these secured credit card grantors can be found in papers like the National Inquirer, Star, and Globe. These outfits guarantee to get you a credit card and usually charge a fee of around $30.00 to $50.00.

"Be careful of these offers in the paper because many of them will charge you a referral fee, only to turn your name over to an exclusive firm who will charge you an application fee on top of that and then forward your application to the issuing bank itself for approval."

SIGNATURE LOANS

Here's another passport to success in taking advantage of a good deal or profitable transaction when it passes your way. "Signature loans are your key to the vault." And signature loans (or *character* loans) are just that, loans granted on "your signature" alone. No co-signer or collateral is involved in a real signature loan.

With pen in hand, based on prior credit history and experience with your bank, your signature can draw from $1,000.00 to $250,000.00. It all depends on your ability to pay it back. Even more so than your ability to pay it back, is your "reputation" of paying it back.

Once you get your first signature loan with a bank, walk in on the day it's due, meet with your loan officer, and pay it off with two cashiers checks or two different stacks of money. The first stack of money will be to cover the principal amount of the loan. As you give him this, be sure and tell him how well you did for yourself in renting that money. "I made a lot of money on that loan, Mr. Loan Officer." Tell him not to spend that money because you "might come back to rent it again, so hang on to it for me." As you pay back the interest portion on the loan (the rent), make sure you point out how much money the bank made on the loan. Remind him that the bank made a profit based on your performance on the loan. Make him acknowledge that the bank made money on the loan. Remind him that it's the rent paid on these loans that keep the bank in business.

Now, let's say your loan was for $3,000.00. As you get up to leave the bank, turn to him and say, "Oh, by the way, I may want to rent $5,000.00 in a couple of weeks. Will you hold onto $5,000.00 for me?" What you are doing is pre-qualifying a $5,000.00 loan. You're saying, "Hey, Mr. Loan Officer, are you gonna raise my next signature loan to $5,000.00 or is $3,000.00 the limit?" What can he say? You just paid back the $3,000.00, you paid back the rent, making it perfectly clear that the bank made money on the transaction, and that it's this rent which keeps the doors open and pays his salary. What can he say? If he answers with, "We'll see," sit back down at his desk and say, "You mean you're not sure? What seems to be the problem?"

Get a commitment on the next loan from him in advance. He won't answer with the word "yes," but a "sure" or "I suppose" will suffice. Don't leave the bank until he commits to the next loan. With each new loan, raise the amount $2,000.00 or so until you're getting signature loans of $10,000.00 at which time you'll start raising future loans in $5,000.00 and $10,000.00 increments.

"When shopping for aggressive banks, ask the person you're dealing with if they are a 'commissioned' loan officer. They are the most aggressive loan officers of all, because they get paid a commission on all the loans they write. These people will be more eager to make you a loan."

Another rule of thumb in renting money is to always ask to rent more money than you want. Here's why. Let's say you want $10,000.00 to purchase a home that needs repairs which will return you a nice profit upon resale. If you need $10,000.00 to successfully complete the transaction, ask for $15,000.00. Providing you receive the entire $15,000.00, you then have $5,000.00 to put in reserve or play with on another project. Now if the loan officer says he can only give you $12,000.00, say, "That will be just fine; that's what I really had in mind anyway." Now if he says the $15,000.00 is a little too much, but that he will loan you $10,000, say, "Fantastic! I was just going to recommend that; you stole the words right out of my mouth."

Had you originally asked for $10,000 and he made a counter offer of $8,000.00, you would come up $2,000.00 short of your needs. It's always easier to "come down" than it is to "go up". **"Always ask for more than you really want or need."** We don't always get what we want, but in most cases, we seem to always get what we need.

CREATIVE CREDIT TECHNIQUES

Here are some ways of building credit or obtaining financing in special situations.

In applying for a real estate mortgage, if your credit reports are bad, or if you don't earn enough income, or if it cannot be verified, there are several solutions to this problem. If your credit reports are full of black marks which would prevent you from obtaining a real estate loan, one way of getting around this is to watch for homes that have an FHA or VA assumable loan on them. For these types of mortgages, there is no qualifying; you just pay a $50.00 assumption fee and anyone can assume these loans. This method of purchasing a home allows even the person with the worst credit to buy a home. All they need is the down payment.

Another way to get around having to have good credit to purchase a home is to find one that you can buy on the terms of *"subject to"* rather than *"assume"* when it comes to purchasing a home with an existing mortgage on it.

For example: You find a home that you want to purchase, the asking price is $75,000.00 with only $5,000.00 down, and assume present financing. The owner now is firm on his price; in fact he's more concerned with getting his asking price than with how you take over the existing financing. Your proposal to him would be, "OK, I'll give you the $75,000.00 you're asking for on the house, and I'll give you the $5,000.00 down payment you request, but you'll have to do one thing for me, Mr. Owner. What's that? Well, it may prevent me from buying your home if I have to go in and qualify for assuming your loan because I have a few little black marks on my credit from a recent divorce (or what have you). But if I can buy this home subject to the terms and conditions of your loan, then we have a deal and can start the closing process."

He'll usually say yes to this kind of offer, if you're honest and sincere with him. When the deal closes, his name is still on the loan but the title goes in your name and you make payments to the seller and then the seller cuts a check to the lender. Rather than doing a "formal assumption" of the loan, you bought the home "subject to" the mortgage's terms and conditions.

Now there are some things that can go wrong with this approach. One would be that some mortgages contain a "due on sale" clause; if the lender finds out the home was sold, he can demand that the entire loan be paid. Most prudent lenders won't call it "due" but they may ask that you sign a new mortgage with them. If you're paying your payments on time, they'll generally let you slide, especially when there's only a little equity behind their loan. It would be foolish to call that loan "due" if you're making the payments on time; the last thing they want is to have that house back. For further information on this matter, consult a competent real estate broker.

Another way to qualify for a home loan if you presently have bad credit or insufficient income is to bring in what's called a "straw buyer."

Let's say you've only been on the job for six months, or you're self-employed and cannot provide proof of income. You want to buy a home; maybe you can't afford the monthly payments. Maybe you can afford the monthly payments but you can't seem to raise the down payment. Here's where a "mouse" meets an "elephant." You're the mouse, you can't raise the down payment but you know a person (an elephant) who has the money just sitting in the bank but that person does not have time to search for real estate investments, and furthermore, he doesn't want the headaches of being a landlord. Here's your proposal: "Ok, Mr. Business Man (or Mr. Doctor, or Mr. Anyone with money), I have this home over on Main Street that I want to buy as an investment, and also as a home for my family and I to live in. I can afford the monthly payments but I don't have the down payment. They want $10,000.00 down, but I just don't have it. Why don't you make the down payment, and I'll make the monthly payments. I'll also do all the maintenance and upkeep at my expense; we can split the cost of any major repairs over $500.00 which may occur. We'll keep the house for five years at which time we'll sell it and split the profit." This is called "profit participation." It was also known as "equity share" until the IRS began to scrutinize this term and procedure.

These types of transactions are created and take place everyday of the year. It's nothing new; it's just a form of being creative with credit. You'll have to do further research on the nuts and bolts of these methods if you're interested in utilizing them.

Now, let's say there is a nice home you'd like to buy, you can raise the down payment but the monthly payments are a little bit more than you can handle. Let's say the payments on this new home are $800.00 monthly, but you're presently leasing an apartment for $600.00 a month and that's about all you can afford.

Tell the elephant that you will make the down payment on the home, live in it, do the maintenance and upkeep if he'll put in $200.00 towards the house payment each month. At the end of five years, you'll sell it and split the profits.

Once again, why would anyone want to shell out $200.00 a month for house payments, or $10,000.00 for a down payment on a home he's not even gonna live in? Well, two reasons: Number one is for future profit (that home is most likely going to increase in value in five years) and, number two, is the tax benefits that are available with owning investment property.

The big Hyatt and Hilton Hotels? Hyatt doesn't buy those buildings outright; a group of investors pool their money to build those fancy buildings and then hires a management company to run it. Hyatt or Hilton is only the franchisor here and you probably thought that Hyatt paid to have those buildings built. No, it's "profit participation." It's being done every day on anything from single family homes to shopping malls and office buildings. Why can't you be creative and structure a deal like one of these?

In business, it's Leverage Buy Outs (LBOs). A couple of years ago, in one of the major business newspapers, there was an article about three men who teamed up and bought an 1100 room Holiday Inn with "no cash down." LBOs are taking place every day. Basically what happens is that you purchase a business, using the business' assets and cash flow as a means to finance the deal.

Be creative with credit and always keep in mind that if there's a will, there's a loan; you just have to find it. If you can't find it, create it!

Any time you create a void or a vacuum, it must be filled with something, somehow. If you take a bucket of water out of the ocean, the ocean fills the hole up with water again. The same hold true for creating a loan when you can't find one. Providing you have the need and the will to do it, you'll get it somehow. Create a void, commit to that void and watch it fill itself.

If *broke countries* can borrow millions and billions of dollars, then why can't you obtain the financing you need?

CHECKING ACCOUNTS AND "OVERDRAFT PROTECTION"

Here's another form of a "no questions asked line of credit," somewhat similar to a Visa card, providing you want it. This form of credit which can be added to the checking accounts of qualified individuals is called Overdraft Checking Protection. But before we go into depth on this, let's cover the general information about checking accounts themselves.

To begin with, checking accounts can be a real pain if you don't have a good record keeping system.

They should be kept as clean as a whistle. Don't bounce any checks on the account. If you find yourself bouncing a check every now and then, go open up another account and never bounce even one check on it. You need at least one clean checking account to use as a reference on your credit applications. Prospective creditors may verify the account you list. They'll be looking for your demonstration of "responsibility and stability." They'll ask your bank whether or not you bounce checks (responsibility) and how long the account has been opened (stability).

One thing you'll want to do when your monthly statement and canceled checks come back, is to make sure that the bank has all of their figures correct. Looking at your statement alone won't do it. Next to your account number on the bottom of your canceled check, in the far right hand corner is the actual amount the bank debited your account. Make sure that amount matches the amount you wrote in the box. Usually they're pretty accurate about this but it's a good idea to double check their figures.

"Some banks offer a "safe check keeping" service where they will store all your checks for you. But it's best to get your checks sent back to you each month. It could take days, perhaps weeks, for them to retrieve a check if you ever needed it to show proof of payment on an account. Plus they'll charge a fee to retrieve the check. Even worse is that you can barely read the damned thing when they make a copy from microfiche!"

They already have a photocopy of the front and back sides of every check. They don't need the checks themselves. They maintain these check photos on microfiche in case the IRS wants to monitor or audit your check writing activities. This government of ours is in on everything we do.

CARRY SOME CASH

By the year 2000, the IRS should be able to tell you exactly what 95% of your income was spent on. We are moving into the Electronic Age. They want to keep tabs on every dime we earn and spend, and what we spend it on. They eventually want to do away with cash altogether. All these electronic banking systems that some of you people think are so neat, are going to be used to monitor your life in the future. It won't be so cool when the government can punch your name into a computer and recall more information on you than you can remember yourself, right down to how many candy bars you consume. Think about it. The federal government already has 3.2 billion files on us, that's equal to 18 files on each.

Get back to carrying cash while there's still cash to carry. Some of you people write a check for a lousy loaf of bread. You have the checkout stands in the grocery stores all tied up! Next time you find yourself becoming impatient while standing in line at the checkout stand, start looking around and see what people are using to pay for their purchases. What are you paying with? Start carrying some cash with you. Some of you can hardly even remember what cash looks like. If it weren't for the game shows on TV, you probably wouldn't remember what color the ink was.

"If you're afraid of getting mugged, that's all the more reason to carry cash. Those little bandits aren't gonna stand around waiting for you to cut them a check for $50.00. They want and need cash; that's why you're being mugged."

Here are a few special situations that may occur with having a checking account. First of all, you know about bouncing checks. The average fee on a NSF check is $10.00 but you'll see that raised to $15.00 before you know it. You can be sure the bankers will whine some more about losing money when you bounce a check on their bank, before they raise the NSF charge to $15.00, but you'll see it happen shortly. They used to raise this fee in one dollar increments. But now they raise it in

$5.00 increments. After $15.00 comes $20.00 and then $25.00, and so on down the line.

When a check bounces, you'll be charged the set NSF fee. If you deposit before the check hits your bank a second time, you save another NSF charge. If they do run it through twice and it bounces twice, then you pay twice. The merchant you wrote the check to can also charge you a fee if the check is returned a second time unpaid. If it bounces twice, the merchant can send it in for collection with your bank. Your bank then sits on the check until you deposit some money again.

"Stop payment" on a check is done at your branch office. It usually costs about $6.00 or $7.00 to do it. They'll raise that fee to $10.00 before we know it, too.

Providing they haven't paid a check of yours before you contact them, you can demand that they stop payment on that check. Many times it's hard to convince a merchant that the blender you purchased from him was defective before you used it. Some will be reluctant to exchange the merchandise or make a refund. Providing your bank didn't pay the check yet, you can give yourself the refund by stopping payment on the check. You can later discuss whether the merchandise was defective before you bought it or not. This puts you in a position to settle the matter fairly.

Lost or stolen checks should be reported to your bank immediately. This way they will do a signature check before paying on your checks and avoid any possible forgeries.

Never write a check out to cash and carry it with you or leave it lying around. Anyone can cash it and you won't have any recourse on being reimbursed for it.

If you should ever buy a "cashier's" check, don't lose it! They are nearly impossible to stop payment on. Instead, buy "association" checks drawn on your bank.

A lost "cashier's" check requires a 90 day waiting

period before you're able to purchase a bond which is required in most cases to be reimbursed on the lost check. And even then, you're still liable to the bonding company, should anyone find and cash it in the future.

OPENING NEW ACCOUNTS

Whenever you open a new checking account, take control of the situation. Bank personnel who open new accounts are trained to start your check numbers at 100. Don't let them start you with such a low number. Many merchants won't even accept a check under 500. Request that you be started at 1000 or 1500. This will help in cashing checks.

You need a checking account for two simple reasons. First, you need it as a reference and for scoring points on your credit applications. Secondly, these checking accounts can later be turned into an unsecured line of credit, or a "no questions asked" loan.

Overdraft Protection is the name of this line of credit involving the use of a checking account. It will show up on your credit reports as a "revolving account" which is a strong piece of credit to have as a reference for future credit. Credit lines on these can vary with each person. The minimum amount is $300.00. The maximum? The sky's the limit; there really are no bounds. It just depends on your ability to pay it back.

As with your Visa or Mastercard, this, too, is a revolving account which means you can pay your billing in full or in convenient monthly payments. If you want to establish a lot of unsecured credit, this is a good way to achieve your goal.

"Some institutions offer an overdraft protection service which draws funds out of your savings account, but this is not a genuine form of overdraft protection. All this is, is a funds transfer service. Any bank in town will transfer funds

from one account to the next, but how many will give you a sole and separate, unsecured, "no questions asked" line of overdraft protection? Deal with those who want to do 'business'!"

PREPARING A FINANCIAL STATEMENT

Financial statements are a two-part system. First, there's the **"Income and Expense Statement"**, and then there's the **"Balance Sheet."** The balance sheet will reveal what your true worth is (financially). If you sold everything you own today (assets) and used that money to pay off every debt you have (liabilities), how much would you end up with? The figure you arrive at is what's called your *net worth*. That's how much you're really worth in dollars and cents.

The income and expense statement is what's used to list all the sources of income you may have coming in. On the opposite side of the sheet you would list all of your expenses. This is how a budget is developed. The income and expense statement can be used to target areas where expenses can be reduced. By listing all your income on one side of the paper and all your expenses on the other, after deducting your expenses from your income, this figure you arrive at is called *cash flow*. A positive cash flow means you end up with money after the expenses are subtracted from the income, and a negative cash flow means you're in trouble. It means that your expenses are greater than your income.

Income/expense statements can be drawn up monthly, quarterly, bi-annually or annually. It's a good idea to do one on yourself or your business at least every six months so that you can monitor your progress and where you're going financially.

You will probably be listing two different types of expenses on your statement. They are *fixed expenses* and *variable expenses*. Fixed expenses are payments you know of in advance and the exact amount like rent, mortgage or car payments, etc. Variable expenses are items such as food, gas, telephone, baby-sitter, etc. To arrive at your variable expenses, just average out what those items have cost you per month over the last six or twelve months.

You can get a standard copy of the balance sheet and income and expense statement from any bank. It's wise to fill out both as completely as you can, just so you know where you are financially. Also, save them over the years so you can chart your progress with what your financial goals in life have been versus what you actually achieved. These two forms that make up your financial statements are a "direct reflection" of your financial position in life.

INCOME AND EXPENSE STATEMENT

FROM ________________ TO ________________

INCOME

Gross Salary	$_____
Minus Deductions	_____
Net Take Home	_____
Other Income	_____
Minus Deductions	_____
Net Other Income	_____
Gifts (Cash)	_____
Commissions	_____
Bonus/Tips	_____
Alimony/Child Support	_____
Business Income	_____
Professional Income	_____
Rental Property Income	_____
Net Profit from Sale of Merchandise	_____
Refunds/Rebates incl. Income Tax	_____
Income from Trusts	_____
Life Insurance Benefits	_____
Disability	_____
Social Security	_____
Royalties	_____
Unemployment	_____
Veterans Benefits	_____
Pensions	_____
IRAs/Keoghs	_____
Other	_____
Total Income	$_____
Total Expenses	$_____
Cash Flow Available	$_____

EXPENSES

Mortgage Payment	$_____
Rent	_____
Other Property	_____
Utilities	_____
Food/Household Goods	_____
Transportation	_____
House Maintenance	_____
Auto Maintenance	_____
Insurance	_____
Installment Contracts	_____
Credit Card Payments	_____
Property Taxes	_____
Income Taxes	_____
Other Taxes	_____
Self-Improvement	_____
Personal Care Items	_____
Entertainment	_____
Lease Payments	_____
Alimony/Child Support	_____
Savings Program	_____
Charity Contributions	_____
Dues/Memberships	_____
Medical Expenses	_____
Child Care	_____
Other	_____
Total Expenses	$_____

BALANCE SHEET

FROM ______________ TO ______________

ASSETS
(Present Market Value)

Cash on Hand	$_____
Savings	_____
Checking	_____
Real Estate	_____
Time Deposits	_____
Vested Pension	_____
Automobiles	_____
Other Vehicles	_____
Accounts Receivable	_____
Notes Receivable	_____
Life Insurance (Cash Value)	_____
Stocks/Bonds/etc.	_____
IRAs/Keoghs	_____
Rebates/Refunds	_____
Other Assets	_____
Tools and Equipment	_____
Antiques/Art/Jewelry	_____
Home Furnishings	_____
Patents/Trusts	_____
Other Interests	_____
Other Assets	_____
Total Assets	$_____
Less Liabilities	$_____
Net Worth	$_____

LIABILITIES
(Total Amount You Owe)

Real Estate Mortgages	$_____
Taxes	_____
Notes Payable	_____
Accounts Owed	_____
Contracts Owed	_____
Other Debts Owed	_____
Total Liabilities	$_____

(Subtract Liabilities from Assets to determine Net Worth)

PART FIVE

SMART CREDIT MANAGEMENT

In managing the credit you now have or plan to get in the near future, there are some "red flags" you'll want to be sure and watch for. These are advanced warning signals that you could be getting in over your head and not even know it. Become familiar with these credit check-points just so you'll recognize some of the events that take place prior to a person's financial situation taking a turn for the worse. You don't want all of your hard-earned credit to start running backwards on you. Credit is much too precious for that. Engrave these safety principles on the front of your mind so as to avoid credit problems in the future.

First of all, if you run out of money before payday, you're probably already in trouble and don't know it. Secondly, if you juggle bills or rob Peter to pay Paul, there could be a problem being created that you need to examine. **"A trap many fall into is using cash advance features from Visa and Mastercard to pay everyday living expenses. The heart of this problem is very clear: 'too much spending and not enough income.'"**

If you find yourself charging more on your accounts than the amount you pay on those balances each month, a storm could be brewing. If you find yourself accepting pre-approved credit card promotions being sent to you when things are already a little tight, this could cause a major problem. If you receive late notices on any of your bills or if you find yourself paying the "late fee" on your rent or home mortgage payment, then there could be danger. If you find yourself racing to the bank and making a deposit to cover checks, chances are very good that you're getting over-extended.

"All credit accounts have limits on them which were once based on your income and ability to pay. As you obtain more and more accounts, your indebtedness usually increases and you find yourself paying out more than what's coming in or at least trying to anyway."

What we need to do is set our own *personal credit limits* that will allow us enough money to pay all our bills and living expenses, plus tuck a few bucks away. You can raise your personal limit as your income increases but you must also allow for the rise in the cost of living each year as well.

You're capable of figuring out what your own personal credit limit should be by working out the numbers on a set of financial statements. Once you've arrived at a dollar amount it's then your responsibility to stay within your limit. Discipline your spending habits so that your habits work for you versus you working for your habits.

Managing credit is quite simple providing you set some personal credit limits and stay inside them.

WHAT TO DO WHEN DEBTS PILE UP

What should one do when debts pile up? Call your creditors and explain your situation. This is hard to do sometimes and the creditors realize this, but they'll usually cooperate with you in lowering your payments or something of that nature. Don't wait to call your creditors after your accounts has been turned over to collections; call them as soon as you see the problem develop. A creditor with any sense at all would rather receive a partial payment than no payment at all.

"The mistake most people make is that they wait for their creditors to start calling them. It may be too late then. They seem to get madder with each day that passes without you calling them."

Many times, providing you call your creditors as soon as a problem develops, the creditor, let's say a department store, will tell you to stop charging until the final balance has been satisfied. But if you wait 30 or 60 days for them to call, then chances are very good that they'll close your account and turn it over for collection while the bill is still fresh.

Most creditors will deal with you but it's up to you to initiate the first phone call. It's better to have a creditor stop you from charging, and eventually reinstate your account than it is to have your account *closed at grantor's request*. Accounts closed at grantor's request have a negative effect on your credit reports.

"When debts pile up, most people will stir and worry, many will suffer from sleepless nights, tension, upset stomach and racked nerves. The first solution that comes to mind is bankruptcy. Some will carry it beyond that to suicide. Don't get yourself all worked up about it. Far too many people get all bent out of shape when a financial tragedy sets in."

Put things in their proper perspective. In the first place, the sheriff won't come and take you away. Secondly, it's only temporary, this won't go on forever; it will soon be solved. Thirdly, this experience will make you become a much bigger, better and wiser person if you live up to its challenge. And fourthly, in every adversity, there's a seed of equal or greater benefit, and something good can happen because of this!

Everyone at some point in their lives will encounter some degree of financial challenges to deal with at least once. Ask yourself if this *problem* will break you, or will you break it? The *problem* doesn't care. It doesn't care if you solve it or if you stew and worry over it. One way or another, the *problem* realizes that its position is only temporary.

It's now just a matter of how you're gonna solve the *problem*, but the *problem* doesn't care how you solve it; it just knows it will be solved. The *problem's* replacement then is the *solution.* The *solution* offers many creative avenues to take. The *solution* says you can file bankruptcy or get a debt consolidation loan or make arrangements to pay partial payments or not pay at all. The *solution* doesn't care which avenue you take; the *solution* is only here to complement the problem.

In every problem there's at least a dozen solutions. There's usually many things you can do to turn your situation in a more positive direction.

"When debts pile up, the first priority in almost any case is to protect your credit as much as possible." A lot of people want to run out and file bankruptcy when their finances turn sour. Nine times out of ten it's highly recommended to stay away from bankruptcy. Bankruptcy is a last resort solution; your right to file bankruptcy should be reserved for that moment when you're faced with "no way out" but to file. There's usually another way out other than bankruptcy.

When debts pile up, it's often necessary to look for ways to cut out any spending for the "unnecessary niceties" of life like cable TV, movies, sporting events, hobbies, etc. No one likes being deprived of these things but realize in advance that it's only temporary.

"If you have debts piling up, find some things you are not using and sell them to relieve some of your debt. A good rule of thumb to follow is: If you have an item which you haven't used in the last six months and don't plan to use in the next three months, sell it!"

People are afraid to let go of some things that inevitably hold them back. It's very difficult getting to second base if you don't take your foot off of first base. Nobody wants to lose status or prestige, and no one wants to go backwards in life, but it's amazing the number of people who go down with a sinking ship, only to lose something they probably could have sold to begin with.

If you have an uneasy feeling that your car is going to get repossessed, sell it before it does, and not only will you pay the debt off but you just might have enough money left over to buy a less expensive automobile that will serve your purpose until you can afford a newer car later.

Don't let your pride get in the way. Pride will cause you to fight it and you'll probably eat up any equity you have in it with repossession and legal fees. You'll probably end up with an *involuntary repossession* on your credit report and absolutely no cash out of the transaction.

"There's a large number of people who lose their homes due to foreclosure. Some of these homes have substantial equity factors in them and most people really are unaware of what to do in a foreclosure situation but common sense would tell them to discount the home 10% to 20% of its value and sell it before it's taken back by the lender."

We all know that the real estate market goes into a slump sometimes when the interest rates are high. But there's always a market for real estate when there's a good deal to be had. There is almost always a buyer to be found for "discounted" real estate property.

It's quite obvious that when a problem occurs, like debts piling up, something needs to be changed. Maybe you need more income or maybe it's just to decrease your spending a little bit.

"Many people believe that just making more money will cure their financial difficulties, but this theory won't hold water in most instances."

There are people who make six-digit incomes that get behind on their payments. You may wonder how a person earning $100,000.00 per year can run short on spendable income but they do, it happens every day; they just spend more than they make, that's all.

Big wage earners buy big ticket items that come with big monthly payments and, yes, of course, they face big problems when they get over-indebted or the source of their income dries up.

In most cases, to increase your income is not the complete answer to your financial problems because you'll just spend whatever more you earn. The real answer to your problem is in controlling how much you spend. It's not usually your "income" that gets you in trouble financially: it's your "expenditures" that cause the problem. And then there will be emergencys that arise.

If you work for someone else and receive an hourly wage, then it may be a good idea to design a workable budget and limit yourself accordingly, whereas if you work on commission or have your own business, you can usually drum up enough new business to increase your income if you have a couple of months of excessive spending. In either case, just watch what you spend and you'll be Ok.

If you ever find yourself with more bills than you have

money for, stop charging on your credit cards; put them away or cut most of them up, however, hang on to one or two major cards to maintain some open credit accounts. Many times people will cut up "all their credit cards" only to have to re-apply in the future at which time their credit reports are reflecting bad ratings from the crisis they recently experienced.

Finally, stop buying on impulse! Leave your credit cards at home when you're out mall walking. Sleep on it a few days before making any large purchases. In most cases, you'll find that you really didn't need that new dress or that new riding-type lawn mower with the chrome wheels and in-dash stereo system.

Don't let anything here discourage you from "increasing" your income. Just watch what you spend, put some money aside in savings and your financial problems in life will be minimal.

DEBT CONSOLIDATION

Shall I consolidate or shall I not? If you do, take precautions. Although many companies claim to help solve your debt problems, some of these firms will only create new ones for you.

"Woe be to those who turn their money over to an "it's-in-the-mail" debt consolidation company. These firms end up taking extensive Caribbean vacations at your expense. You must be careful in choosing a reputable consolidation company." Scores of people have been burned by these "Congratulations" companies. "Congratulations, you're our next sucker." If there's a business opportunity that has a free lunch to offer, it has to be the "Congratulations" business.

"In deciding which consolidation company to do business with, it's recommended that you first

call Consumer Credit Counselors. They have over 200 officers in 44 states. Best of all, they are a 'non-profit' organization and the fees they charge are very minimal. Contact them prior to any other consolidation firm."

There are some companies out there that will provide a clean-cut, honest service, but you cannot afford to find out which one it is if you're already having a problem paying your bills. These firms may charge anywhere from 15 to 35% of the funds you give them to pay your bills, as their fee. The idea here is to get out of debt versus creating another expenditure, an expensive one at that.

Consumer Credit Counselors (CCC) are supported by contributions from the business community. When you contact them you'll be mailed a standard budget form to list all your debts and income. You must complete this form before they can analyze your financial situation. To start with they'll look for areas to trim your expenses, possibly enough to cover all your debts depending on your own individual situation. If, after trimming the fat from your life-style, you still come up short on funds to cover your debts, CCC may then recommend a debt management program.

Providing you and your creditors approve, CCC will design a game plan in which everyone will be satisfied, often times asking creditors for extensions or to lower or even drop the interest or finance charges altogether so that you can get back on your feet and the creditors can get at least the principle balance paid back to them.

Providing all parties involved approve of this plan, CCC will require that you pay them a set amount each month, which they will administer accordingly to your various creditors. You must also agree not to take on any more debt until this matter has been resolved; you'll probably find it difficult to get credit anyway.

All counseling sessions are free, however, there is a small minimal fee to cover some of the costs of the debt management programs. In a hardship case there is no fee at all. How can you beat a deal like this? CCC won't absorb 15% to 35% of your money as a profit to them. And this is not bankruptcy.

"Many Congratulations companies will reel you in on something called a Debt Relief Program or a Debt Reorganization Plan which is usually just a toned-down phrase for Chapter 13 Bankruptcy."

Some businesses will advertise that they make *consolidation loans*. These loans can often be helpful and cost effective but you really need to watch what you're doing.

"Some of the biggest crimes known to mankind have been committed with paper and ink. Many times in the fine print of a loan agreement, your house will be attached as collateral. Be very careful what you get yourself into. You could wind up living on Skid Row."

Consolidation loans are best used when they're applied for when all your payments are "current." You're then in a much better position to entertain the possibilities of a consolidation loan because your mind is clear and generally more open to spotting any unfavorable terms such as using your home as collateral.

A loan such as this can also have many benefits to it. Normally, the interest rates on credit cards are pretty steep, 21% on some Visa cards. If you have several credit cards with high interest rates, it's sometimes wise to get one big loan at a lower interest rate to pay off all your high interest rate accounts. Once again, be careful with anything that looks like a good deal because it could have hidden costs that would eat up any savings on lower interest rates. It could actually end up costing you more than you thought you were saving.

If your bills are backing up and you're considering whether or not to get a consolidation loan, call Consumer Credit Counselors and talk your situation over with them first. They could save you a lot of trouble and perhaps some money, too. Look in the Appendix for the address of the CCC office nearest you.

MANNER OF PAYMENT

Understanding how the Manner of Payment affects your credit reports is very important. Manner of Payment (M.O.P) simply means, the manner in which you pay your bills. Do you pay on time as agreed or are you sometimes 30, 60, 90, or 120 days late?

"Manner of Payment is important to lenders. They want to know how you're going to pay. They want and expect the money owed them on or before the due date."

Lenders and merchants approving new credit applications will check your credit reports to see how you've paid your bills in the past. They won't overlook the M.O.P. on your other accounts, you can be sure of that. Why? Simply because creditors understand that we are creatures of habit. Our M.O.P. in the past is usually a good reflection of what our M.O.P. might be like in the future. People can and do change their habits but lenders are skeptical and pessimistic towards people's ability to make such a change. They believe that the "old" you is the "present" and "future" you. They don't really believe you'll ever change.

"If you owe a debt you are obligated to pay it and preferably 'on time as agreed' or 'late' if you must, just so long as you satisfy the debt."

On the other hand, it's foolish to ruin your credit when things go wrong with your finances and like most everyone, you too will probably have some financial challenges in life. So why not learn "who to pay late" where it will show up and hurt you the least; if it even hurts you at all?

WHO TO PAY LATE

Knowing who to pay late, in advance of meeting face-to-face with a financial crises, is very important to the maintenance of clean credit reports. *These principles are not to be used in "burning" some of your creditors, but only to be used in the event that "someone must get paid late."*

There are countless reasons why one might be late in paying their bills; it happens to everyone at one time or another. For some people, there is usually plenty of cash to pay bills with, but writing a check and putting it in the mail is always last on their list. **"Anyone who habitually pays their bills late, whether it's due to a lack of funds to work with or just plain neglect on your part (you've not placed a value on your credit yet), then there is a cancerous growth on your reports, and it's spreading. In other words, it's loading up with 'black marks.'"**

In the eyes of a lender, your credit reports are your "soul," and each black mark represents a "credit sin." Worst of all, it takes a long time to be "born again," and washed of your sins, so to speak.

In some credit reports like TRW and Trans Union, there is a column provided for recording your Manner of Payment. It will list what your last 12 months of payment activity has been. A "C" on your TRW means you are current. A straight line of "C"s look great, but a "1" means you were 30 days late, a "2" means 60 days late, a "3" stands for 90 days, "4" means 120 days, "5" means 150 days and "6" means 180 days. (All the codes will be supplied with each individual report.) Here's how it will look on your TRW:

	M.O.P.											
	1	2	3	4	5	6	7	8	9	10	11	12
B of A **Paid as Agreed** **30 ( ) 60 ( ) 90 ( )**	C	C	C	C	C	C	C	C	C	C	C	C
Sears **Current was 90** **30 ( ) 60 ( ) 90 (5)**	C	C	3	3	3	3	3	C	C	C	C	C
Wards **Current was 60** **30 ( ) 60 (5) 90 ( )**	C	2	2	C	2	C	2	2	C	C	C	C

Some people will argue that they already have plenty of credit so it doesn't matter what their reports reflect because they don't need any more credit. But they may need clean credit in the future, whether they believe it or not. A person could get a "job transfer" and be forced to sell his home in order to buy a new one. Maybe, there's a "balloon payment" coming due in a few years on your home mortgage that you forgot about having to pay off or refinance. Maybe you're in the market for a "new job."

Many large corporations will pull your credit reports to help determine whether or not you're a responsible person. Potential employers pull job applicant's credit reports and so do a lot of insurance companies before writing a new policy. Your car could be stolen or wrecked in an accident causing you to apply for a new car loan. Your home could be damaged or demolished forcing you to buy a new one. Anything can happen, and when it does you'll probably need some credit reflecting a good manner of payment in order to get financed. **"Maintaining a good credit profile nowadays is nearly as important as is maintaining good health!"**

When you've received a copy of each credit report from the CRAs in your area, look at each to see how some merchants have supplied information on two or three reports whereas other creditors with whom you have credit didn't report at all.

"Rule number one in paying someone late is to pay someone who doesn't report!"

Who are you making a payment to who is not on your credit report? Is the phone company on any of your reports? Is the gas and electric company? Is the jeweler, the corner hardware store, the oil company (Texaco, Shell, Mobil, etc.)? Is your landlord reporting? Your home mortgage company? Utility companies don't usually report your credit to the CRAs unless it's a collection account. They will, however, shut your utilities off if you don't pay them, but then it's much better to receive a late notice from them than from Diners Club or J. C. Penney. Utility companies will usually give you an "extension" to pay your bill late if you call and make arrangements. They're generally pretty flexible.

Many small merchants you now have credit with may not be reporting. It doesn't pay for them to report. Oil companies don't usually report, nor do mortgage companies. You would think that your house payment would be reported each month, but that's rare unless it's a second mortgage or home improvement loan by a commercial lender, and even then it's very rare.

Landlords don't report the M.O.P. of your rent because; it doesn't pay to do it. As far as that goes, it would be much wiser to pay your rent a few days late versus paying an account late who is reporting.

"What's 'late'? Late is when a curious creditor calls and you tell him 'it's in the mail.' That's late! Late is one day after the due date."

Many bank loans still have a "grace period." If your car payment with Chase Manhattan is due on the 1st but you're given 15 days grace, then by paying it by the 15th, your late but there is no late fee and it won't be reported as late. If you wait until the 16th to pay it, then you're "late-late" and there will usually be a late fee, and it will most likely be reported to the CRAs and show up on your reports, not as being one day late but as 30 days late because that's what the billing cycles are: 30, 60, 90, 120, etc. Although you might have been only one day late, or one day past the due date, it still shows up as 30 days late.

Credit card companies usually report your manner of payment every month. People will usually pay a credit card late versus a house payment for fear of losing their home, whereas the worst a credit card company could do is garnish some of your wages. Since this is true, prospective creditors can see in advance if you're about to go under or are already buried in debt and this new $5,000.00 loan you're applying for, that you claim is for "continued education," is actually to pay other bills. They don't want to deal with anyone who is about to go belly-up!

Now if you are short on cash and your credit card payments are current, but you need $5,000.00 to pull your house out of foreclosure, the creditor is more likely to give you a new loan. He doesn't know your home is in foreclosure by reading your credit reports because your mortgage company is not reporting. The only other protection for the creditor would be to call and verify your mortgage payments being current, and they hardly ever do this.

"Most lenders look at your TRW, or major credit report, call to verify your employment, and then cut you a check. In today's fast times and easy credit, it's surprising that more financial institutions aren't going Bankrupt! They loan out money very loosely, in many cases, based on clean credit

reports and a source of income to verify if they even bother to verify that!"

Clean credit reports should carry considerable emphasis here, and knowing who to pay late when you must is one of the keys to your success in this crazy world of credit.

With this in mind, in the event you don't even have enough money coming in to pay your accounts which are reporting, much less the ones who don't report, there is still something you can do to save your credit to a large degree. If your credit profile contains more than one report, there is still some hope.

Example; in Southern California there are three major CRAs being TRW, Trans Union (TU) and CBI. TRW is the largest and most commonly used. Trans Union follows TRW in size and usage, and then CBI.

Now, if you were to pay a bill late, even outside of having to pay those creditors who don't report late payments, look to your smallest, lesser-used credit report for a merchant who is not on TRW or TU. Do a little study before paying one who reports late payments. Figure out where it will hurt you the least. This might sound like a waste of time but it's well worth the effort.

"A note of caution, if you are current on all your payments but need a few extra bucks for something or another, don't start paying the non-reporters late. It's a bad habit to develop."

COLLECTION AGENCIES AND "UNPAID ACCOUNTS"

Bill collectors supposedly fulfill an important role in our society. They collect millions and millions of dollars each year on delinquent accounts that may otherwise have gone unpaid, for large and small companies alike.

Many of the larger corporations that extend credit

have an "in-house" collection department. These collectors are usually employees of the corporation and work on a "salary" basis. This type of collector will be more controlled and somewhat mild compared to an outside independent collection agency.

Large companies such as Ward's and Sears will restrict their collection employees efforts a little more than the independent collection agencies. Even though you may be the subject of a collection account, Ward's doesn't want you going around bad mouthing their store because it can be bad for business, but the jerk who works for Strong Arms Collection Agency could not care less what you think or say about him or his company. All he's concerned with is that you pay your bill so he gets a paycheck!

"In paying a collection account you'll want to take some caution. First of all, you'll want to see if that collection account appears on any of your credit reports. If it does, it's always best to negotiate (in advance) with the collection agency to remove the negative entry from your reports when payment in full has been made on the account." Each collection agency however, will have their own policy towards such a practice. Some collection agencies will do it and others won't. Some will say they "can't" take it off, but that's like saying they "can't" call you at home!

It seems foolish that a collection agency would put ego and old dusty company policies ahead of profit. If I were the owner of a collection agency, I'd want my accounts to come in and pay off, which, in turn, I'd remove the negative entry from their reports so they could get some more credit to mess up again so that I could have them as an account again. Collection agencies make money on accounts collected, not on ruining credit reports. I guess one of the joys in collecting delinquent accounts is in having the power of putting the "screws" to someone's credit report. What a rotten profession to be in!

Be sure to make any possible arrangements to have negative entries removed upon payment in full on that account. It's best to request a letter to this effect. **"'Paid Collection' looks just as bad as 'Collection Account' in most cases."**

When an account of yours gets turned over to one of those screwballs for collection, you can safely bet that they'll try and get full payment out of you which you may not have. Arrange a payment plan, and get it in writing but really push for having the derogatory entry removed. **"Any mention whatsoever of a collection account on your credit reports, whether paid or not, could very well cause you to be denied future credit priviledges for the next seven years. This is specially true when applying for a new 'unsecured' credit account."**

Some collectors may even "discount" the amount due for fast payment. You may be able to pay $300.00 cash to satisfy a $500.00 bill. Be sure and get a "paid in full" receipt.

"Never make payments on a collection account with your personal checking account because they may record your account number and pull a fast one on you."

With your checking account number and the bank's name (and having a judgment against you), they can call your bank around the normal payday periods: Fridays, the 1st or 15th day of the month and then slap a "lien" on your account which actually freezes a portion of, and sometimes "all" the money in your account. The next thing that happens is that all your checks come marching home (NSF) at your expense!

"Don't ever pay collection accounts with a check

written on your personal account." If you do, then don't deposit anymore funds in that account other than to cover only this check and to keep the account active.

Most bill collectors will even tell you to send them "post-dated" checks. If you owe $300.00 and agree to pay them $100.00 a month for three months, they'll usually try this method. Take caution here; they just might deposit the checks whether they're good or not and then you'll be in even deeper!

In the Appendix you will find a reproduction of the Fair Debt Collection laws. Be sure to review them if you're the subject of a collection account. Know your rights. Bill collectors lay awake at night conniving new methods to get their greedy little paws on your money.

"Remember, professional collectors aren't saints either. Chances are very good that the person who's pouring the coals to you about your delinquent doctor bill just might be trying to catch up on late payments of his own. Don't let these people rain on your parade. Put them in the proper perspective."

THE REPO MAN

The Repo Man is a talented little Devil, he usually works during the wee early morning hours. It never used to make any sense seeing a tow truck pulling a new car which didn't appear to be smashed up, and particularly in the middle of the night. I could understand such an action at that hour had the car just been in an accident. But to see a nice clean, wrinkle-free car being towed at 3:00 or 4:00 a.m. was a bit strange to me. Some repo professionals will drive cars away but the usual method is to hook the car up to a wrecker and tow it.

"People who are expecting a visit from the Repo Man will sometimes try to outsmart him, but the

Repo Man is pretty wise. He sweeps the streets of you neighborhood looking for your car if it's not in your driveway."

Locked garage doors and subterranean parking places won't always stop a determined Repo Man; all he needs to do is "think" he knows where it is and it can be considered repossessed. Its almost like they're *licensed* to steal!

If your car is about to be repossessed, take caution. These guys are slick! And not only in taking the car, but in locating it as well. Repo Men are excellent "skip tracers" when it comes to finding a person who has moved to a new address, whether it is across town or across the country.

To start with, they may send a piece of junk mail to your house with the words "Forwarding Address Requested" in the top left hand corner of the envelope. When the Post Office delivers the letter, and finds your address has been changed, the Postal Service forwards the letter to your new address and then notifies the sender of the forwarding address, being most people file a change of address when they move.

Another way they will find you is by calling your old phone number to get the new number. The first three digits tell what part of town you're in. Then it's just a matter of looking in the proper cross-reference directory and now they have your new address.

They will even use the credit bureau and one of your credit card numbers in a much sneaker way. What they will do is call your credit card companies billing department and rudely ask, "Where's my bill?" The representative will ask for the account number of the bill in question. "It's 3471-0770-1234; what address are you sending it to? Are you still sending it to (subject's old address)?" "No, sir, we sent it to 365 Main Street, Apt. #5 on June 30th." "Oh, I'm sorry, let me check with our apartment manager and see if he may have received it. Thank you. Good bye." Once again they have your new address and it's repo time.

The more talented Repo Men and professional collectors will use some methods even more sophisticated to locate you that I don't even care to mention.

The Post Office has an office which they use to locate people. There is also an office that the Armed Services has to locate people who are in or recently joined the Service, which they often use.

Driver's license bureaus can locate people, too. And the repo man is well aware of this. They have, in each state, an office that will, for just a few dollars, give the driving record of any person plus that person's present address, even if they moved out of state. They can even tell where you were last tagged for a moving violation.

In most cases, if someone wants to find you bad enough, they will. But as it goes with a bill collector's efforts and practices, so goes it with the Repo Man in that many times they will use "illegal" tactics to recover automobiles and other assets.

If you're ever the subject of what looks to be a raw deal, contact an attorney or legal aid and review your case with them. You may be able to recover some money for any damages they may have caused.

CREDITOR'S RIGHTS

Creditors tip the scales over consumers when it comes to each others rights. But then that's only fair in most cases because the creditors stand to lose more in credit transactions than consumers do. That's why, and it's always been a fact of life that: **"He who has the gold makes the rules."** This chapter would be much too lengthy to describe all the various rights State by State, so the following will only be a generalization.

As a rule, creditors can assess late charges for bills paid after the due date. Fortunes are made on late payment penalties. The amount they can charge would be found in the original contract you signed with them.

Creditors can also request you to stop charging on your revolving accounts and if you continue to charge or exceed your credit line limit, they can close the account. Your credit card grantor may also warn other merchants not to accept your card, (some credit reporting bureaus will warn their subscribers if you start showing a pattern of late payments.)

Banks in which you have a line of credit with may pull money out of your checking or savings account to offset late payments on installment loans or lines of credit with them. However, they must leave a certain amount of money in the account which can vary from State to State.

Repossession? Everyone should be aware of the Repo Man by now. Creditors have the right to repossess anything that was used as "collateral" on a now defaulted loan.

Not only can a creditor repossess merchandise which was used to secure a loan but, in some cases, they may also sell the collateral and assess what's called a "deficiency judgment" against you if the *proceeds* from the sale are less than the pay-off amount on the account; should there be any surplus, you would be entitled to it. Should you refuse to turn the property over, they can obtain a court order forcing you to turn it over.

In many states, the merchant must send you a notice that the repossessed item will be sold. The notice will include instructions as to how you can redeem the property. Usually, for a few days, you'll have the right to make full restitution on the loan and get the item back. Some creditors, not many, will let you have the merchandise back if you make up the back payments and pay for any other costs that may have been incurred in repossessing the merchandise.

Many contracts contain what is called an "Acceleration Clause." In the event your contract contains this clause and you get behind even one payment, the creditor then has the right to call the entire balance "due" at once!

Home mortgages are a little more in your favor when they go into default than would be an auto loan or credit line. Each state will have separate foreclosure laws.

Some lenders in states such as California can foreclose on a piece of property in 111 days from the date of filing a Notice of Default with the County Recorder. Other creditors in different states can take from three months to a year to complete a foreclosure. It all depends on the state's regulations and whether the property is secured by a Contract for Deed or a Mortgage.

Creditors can take you to Court and sue. If you don't show up in Court, you would then lose by *default*. Beware of some of the more shady creditors who will often times file their suit in a Court way out in the boondocks somewhere making it difficult for you to appear. Consult a competent attorney if this ever happens to you and also complain to the Court where the case was filed.

If you are sued and the other side wins the case, you are then placed with a *judgment* which states the amount you are to pay the other party. You can pay them on the spot, make arrangements for payment or not pay them at all. However, the plaintiff can have an *asset search* done on you and place a *lien* and force the sale of any property (real estate or personal property) which you may own except for some exemptions allowed you by law. **"It's always best to settle out of court whenever possible. This way you avoid a judgment being reported on your credit reports."**

Wage garnishment is nearly impossible without the prior approval of the Court, however, with the Court's approval, a creditor can garnish wages. The amount they can garnish solely depends upon on each particular case.

The Internal Revenue Service and your State Tax Board can become creditors of yours also. They don't even make you fill out an application or do a credit check to give you credit. They'll give "anyone" credit. Here's how it works: Should the IRS or your State Government ever find that you owe them money on back income taxes, you're given "instant credit." No applications, credit checks or questions asked! They will let you pay the deficiency in full or in monthly payments that fit your budget.

You on the other hand can dispute their claim by filing a petition in Tax Court to have the case reviewed if you feel they are wrong. Now if you do owe them money and they have to come looking for you, first of all they will usually report a *tax lien* on your credit reports and secondly, if you refuse to come to terms with them they can levy a tax lien against any real or personal property you may own and force the sale of that property to satisfy the lien. They can also steal your "income tax returns each year," even for child support payments that are delinquent. The same holds true on student loans that are in default.

Your County Tax Collector will also give you credit. Unpaid property taxes will eventually end up being paid by the sale of your property at auction if you don't pay.

If you ever feel that a creditor may be taking his rights over the line, then look in the white pages of your telephone directory under Consumer Complaint and Protection Coordinators. These Government Offices can be very helpful.

BANKRUPTCY

Bankruptcy (B-K) filings are most common in three basic forms: Chapter 13, 11, and 7.

The Chapter 13 is a debt reorganization plan which, when filed, takes effect immediately, and all collection efforts or foreclosure proceedings must cease. Once the 13 has been filed, the Court allows the person filing it a certain amount of time to draw up a repayment plan for his delinquent accounts. In order to file, you must have a regular source of income. With that amount in mind, whatever it is, you must demonstrate your ability to make your normal monthly payments and make up any back payments within a three year period of time, and up to five years with the Court's permission.

This plan is then submitted to the Bankruptcy Court for approval. When approved, you would then start paying your monthly payments to the Bankruptcy Trustee, who, in turn, pays your creditors and also acts as a mediator between you and your creditors over any questions they may have. You would remain under this plan as long as you continued to pay the trustee, and providing you do not take on any more debt.

The cost to file a 13 is $60.00 and there is also a 10% fee of your total payments which is the trustee's fee. If you have an attorney represent you, his fees are additional. You will retain all your assets providing you complete the plan. If you voluntarily quit paying the trustee, the Chapter 13 will be dismissed. Should you become ill or laid off while on this plan, the trustee may possibly grant an extension if you ask.

This is a good plan to use in most cases where your home is in foreclosure providing you can either make up the missed payments, obtain new financing or make a quick sale and pay off the defaulted mortgage.

As a B-K seasons with time, some "secured" creditors

will overlook it somewhat if you're really solid in all of the other areas of qualifying for credit, like length of time at residence and work, net worth, and ability to pay the payments on this new piece of credit you're out applying for.

Even though as time goes on and the B-K starts losing its power, the fact still remains in the back of their minds that you once filed bankruptcy.

The Chapter 11 Bankruptcy is basically the same as the Chapter 13 but it's used mainly by businesses or individuals who are engaged in business.

As for Chapter 7, this really looks like you burned some creditors. Chapter 7 simply means the Court appoints a trustee to round up all your assets, (less some exemptions) sell them at auction for whatever they can and the proceeds go to pay off all your bills. A Chapter 7 will wipe the slate clean but it leaves a stain on your credit reports for ten years. Chapter 7 is the "last resort;" you really don't want to do this unless it's the only way out.

Avoid a bankruptcy at all costs; they can be quite costly and counterproductive. If you are forced to file a 7 and your case is fairly simple, then you may want to use your local legal service clinic to help you file. The cost to file at present is $90.00. An attorney would charge you anywhere from $500 to $2,000 for the same service your local legal clinic can provide for free.

Should you ever feel that your financial situation in life is "hopeless", don't go running off to a bankruptcy attorney for a quick fix. I've talked with clients who have been told by an attorney that the only way out was bankruptcy, but, after careful review of their situation, we found alternate routes to take and avoided it.

"Not all attorneys are going to have your best interest at heart. Their recommendation for you to file a B-K just might be coming from their pocket-

book versus what would really be to your best interest."

Before seeking the advice of an attorney concerning your financial affairs, contact Consumer Credit Counselors.

Beware of the "want-to-be-lawyers" who engage in coffee shop talk concerning bankruptcy. Many people are fast to recommend filing a B-K, but if you listen to and follow their instructions, you may be in for a rude awakening.

If you've filed a B-K in the past or if you should be forced to file one in the future, don't forget to separate your actions from yourself. Banks experience a form of bankruptcy now and then, too. It's called being "insolvent." And for the past few years, banks have been dropping like flys all around us.

Lending institutions in Texas and Oklahoma have been the hardest hit in this shake-out period where only the strong will survive. The staff of FDIC auditors has grown from two hundred to over two thousand new federal workers in the last six years.

For an even broader view of bank failure look at our federal government who is planning a major bail-out for some 350 Savings and Loans that are so deeply troubled.

As you can see, banks are not perfect either; don't let those expensive TV commercials fool you when they say that **"We're 5 Billion Dollars Strong!"** They don't mention the $5 or $10 billion in weaknesses (liabilities) on the other side of their balance sheet.

Avoid filing a bankruptcy at all costs, it really puts the screws to your credit reports.

Many people still believe that when they file a 7, all the accounts filed on are removed from the credit report, but that's simply not true. When you file a 7, all of your accounts will indicate something to the order of "Charged Off To Bankruptcy" or "B-K Liq. Reo." which means discharged via Chapter 7. The accounts remain on file for 7 years and the bankruptcy remains for 10 years.

CREATING BALANCE

It seems that success in any endeavor requires an "even balance" among all the different substances of which any worthwhile achievement is made up. As for becoming or remaining successful in the world of credit, one must search for that "perfect center" which gives even balance and continued success.

Now, you don't have to go into the depths of "technical analyst" to know where your perfect center is. You know when you're getting in over your head.

To create your perfect balance, fill out a balance sheet and income and expense statement. Understand what your financial position in life is. Next, set your own "personal credit limit" according to what you want and can afford to pay for on credit terms. It would be wise to pay yourself first from each paycheck. Ten percent of your gross income should go into a savings account only to be used for emergency cash and investments, safe investments that can be quickly converted into cash.

"Don't get caught up in all the trappings of life with all these advertisements seen on TV. You'll find that once you bought a product, the thrill or benefit you thought would enhance your lifestyle in one form or another was actually somewhat deceiving and short lived."

Too many people are using credit to purchase a lifestyle they cannot afford. Some people use credit as a "Placebo" (an I shall please). Well, it may pull them out of their depressing state, at the longest, until the time the bill comes in for that purchase.

Another big mistake people make is letting someone charge a purchase on their credit card with them, saying

"I'll pay it back." Many times it doesn't get paid back and you, the account holder, start getting late notices in the mail and even worse, the "Manner of Payment" is being recorded on your credit reports.

It's okay to help out a friend but a more sound method would be to say, "Go ahead an use my card and then pay me back the money plus any finance charges." Now, before giving them the approval to use your card, decide whether or not you can pay for this additional charge if the other person fails to. If you would find it a bit out of reach, then don't give them your credit card to begin with.

It's okay to share your credit info on their reports with them but be careful of letting them make purchases on accounts for which you are contractually liable.

"For those of you who are having financial difficulties right now, whether you're neck deep in debt or just always a day late and a dollar short; your long term 'balance' will only come from raising your self-image."

Most of us were programmed from day one with a lot of negative thoughts about money. We then learned to reaffirm our financial position in life with the words and phrases such as "I'm broke," "I can't afford it," "I'm always late on my car payment," "I don't earn enough money on my job," "I'll always be poor," "I couldn't get a loan if 'God' were to co-sign," etc.

Our mind is the most magnificent computer ever known to mankind. It's made up of a conscious and subconscious mind. At birth out memory banks are blank. With each year that passes, it gets programmed by the society we grow up in. This programing then (which is mostly negative) becomes the program we use to run our lives with. In a nutshell, we are using negative programing and getting back negative results.

All the data that we are exposed to each day passes

through our conscious mind and is stored for future use in our subconscious mind. We hear people use the negative phrases as quoted here. Our conscious mind all the while picks up every word and sends it into that abundant warehouse called the subconscious. Not only do we hear people use all these negative phrases, "but we begin to use them, too!" They start out as flimsy cobwebs at first but grow into steel chains to shackle our lives as the years go by.

Like any series of thoughts that are put into our mind through consistent repetition, the subconscious mind not only begins to believe these suggestions but it also performs the task just as it was designed to do which is to move us towards our currently dominant thoughts.

"We get back what we speak. When we say we are "broke" through a series of repetitions, over a period of weeks, months and years; the subconscious mind sets out to achieve the goal."

Our subconscious mind is a very sophisticated target seeking, goal achieving device. It gets for you (with time allowing) whatever you set before it as a current thought or goal.

If you worry about your bills, your goal is what? "More bills!" If you worry about lack, debt, insolvency, bill collectors, etc., the subconscious mind moves us toward these things and they become a part of our daily lives.

If you worry about something and continue to worry about it and back up your thoughts with equal strength emotions, that which you fear gets even worse and you spend even more time worrying about it until it makes you physically sick! At which point, it drives you to the edge; here's where you say "enough"—there's got to be a *solution*. Now your goal changes from a state of worry and frustration to a new mindset of creative problem solving and scores a direct hit almost everytime and then the once-massive problem is now behind you.

What's all this have to do with creating balance in our financial lives? I'm glad you asked.

"Most everything in our lives originated in the mind first." When ever we worry about something, we must first create the appropriate mental pictures in our mind to give substance to our fear. As we continue to fear a certain event or outcome, we create more negative mental pictures to compliment the ones we are presently using. **"Worry is 'negative' goal setting."**

When we fear loosing our job or going into debt, we create pictures in our imaginations to color in our fear. When we fear being in debt we create a mini series in our mind which is vivid and complete in detail. The more we worry about this certain fear, the clearer it becomes. And then, you wonder why you're always *broke!*

"Based on the experience of scores and scores of the world's top achievers, it's been found that through the process of 'self-imaging' we can create any type of mini series on this continuous loop cassette of ours (which operates our achievement mechanism) and enjoy prosperity using the "same" process we've used to create debt, fear, worry, indecision and frustration."

We can create pictures of being debt free. We can create pictures of having excess cash on hand and in the bank. We can create pictures of paying off the credit cards each month to avoid paying any interest or finance charges. We can create these pictures in our mind of our own free will and with continuous repetition and time allowing, we can create a "perfect balance" in our own personal, world of credit.

Although we cannot erase the last cassette which we used to create the mess we were in (it gets put in storage), we can start a new cassette, a new video, a new mini series in which we can create pictures in our minds, and bring this new motion picture to life!

This practice of self-imaging was formally referred to as the "art of visualization." Neil Armstrong used this visualization process in his practice sessions here on earth to be later used in real life to set foot on the moon.

Tom Watson, Lee Trevino, and Jack Nicklaus all use "self-imaging" as a tool in their profession. These people are "masters" of self-imaging. If they miss a shot on the golf course, they immediately replay the shot in their imagination as a "perfect" shot.

Tennis greats, football stars and Olympic athletes will take some 300 hours of video which views them playing or performing and edit 298 hours of less-than-perfect performance leaving them with a two-hour video of a perfect game. They then view this two-hour video of themselves playing over and over and over again until it's embedded in the subconscious mind and the end result in real life is a perfect game or performance.

Airline pilots are big users of self-imaging whenever they run up against bad weather or adverse conditions. They've been trained to do "mental 180's." This is a half turn, they go back, in their imagination as to when they've flown under the very best of conditions. They imagine flying in perfect conditions as they cut through the storm and land as planned with little or no problem.

Walt Disney used self-imaging. He walked through the once-orange groves in Anaheim, California with an amusement park in "rough draft" on a paper napkin, preplaying in his imagination what has since become Disneyland.

Every top entertainer, athlete, business professional, scientist, inventor, and all the other dynamos in our present day or even as far back as the creation of man, all top achievers have used *self-imaging* to create "extraordinary" events in their lives.

Getting approved is only the first half of establishing credit. Creating balance is the second half,

both must be learned and practiced for you to have continued success in consumer credit.

Creating perfect balance in the world of credit must take place in your *mind* first, before you can ever experience it in real life. No other means will give lasting results until it happens in your mind. What you *see in life* is what you will *be in life.*

All of the answers to life are deep within you. Don't search for an external source for solving life's toughest problems, look within yourself because God is within and he has all the answers.

It's your nature to have perfect balance in every area of your life. There are no limits but the ones you place on yourself. Your peace, joy, harmony and balance in every area of your life should be searched for by consulting your inner self, and then trust in that inner voice and do what it says.

You can have anything you deeply desire and are willing to work towards. It's all yours, you just have to stake your claim. And then go for it!

Thank you.

APPENDIX

CONSUMER CREDIT COUNSELORS SERVICE DIRECTORY

CONSUMER CREDIT COUNSELORS SERVICE DIRECTORY

ALABAMA

CONSUMER CREDIT
COUNSELING SERVICE
OF ALABAMA, INC.
217 S. Court Street, Suite 317
Montgomery, AL 36104
Malda W. Farmer,
Executive Director
(205) 265–8545

ALASKA

CONSUMER CREDIT
COUNSELING SERVICE
OF ALASKA
419 Barrow, Suite A
Anchorage, AK 99501
Myra Hollibaugh,
Executive Director
(907) 279–6501

ARIZONA

CONSUMER CREDIT
COUNSELING SERVICE
OF ARIZONA
3056 N. 33rd Avenue Phoenix,
AZ 85017
John A. Erickson,
Executive Director
(602) 233–0132

Branch Office:
CCCS OF ARIZONA
(LUKE AIR FORCE BASE)
(Appointments made by Base personnel; Military & Base civilians only, 1 day per week)
(602) 856–6791

TUCSON FAMILY DEBT
COUNSELORS
5834 East Speedway Tucson,
Arizona 85712
Raul Lopez,
Executive Director
(602) 747–7850

Branch Office:
TUCSON FAMILY DEBT
COUNSELORS
(SOUTH TUCSON)
(602) 882–9966

ARKANSAS

FAMILY SERVICE AGENCY
CONSUMER CREDIT
COUNSELING SERVICE
P.O. Box 500
North Little Rock, AR 72115
Paul E. Blackstone, ACSW,
Executive Director
(510) 758–1881

CONSUMER CREDIT COUNSELORS SERVICE DIRECTORY

CALIFORNIA

CONSUMER CREDIT
COUNSELORS
ASSOCIATION
OF CALIFORNIA
(State Administrative Office)
31 Geary Street
San Francisco, CA 94108
Frank Sperling,
President
(415) 552–8320 or 552–0665

CONSUMER CREDIT
COUNSELORS
OF KERN COUNTY
1706 Chester Avenue, Suite 320
Bakersfield, CA 93301
Nancy Johnson,
Executive Director
(805) 324–9628

CONSUMER CREDIT
COUNSELORS
OF FRESNO, INC.
2135 Fresno Street, Room 210
Fresno, CA 93721
Ray Willingham,
Executive Manager
(209) 233–6221

CONSUMER CREDIT
COUNSELORS
OF LOS ANGELES
1300 West Olympic, Room 304
Los Angeles, CA 90015
Donna Fong,
Executive Director
(213) 386–7601

Branch Offices:
Baldwin Park, CA
Canoga Park, CA
Gardena, CA
Inglewood, CA
Lakewood, CA
Lancaster, CA
Pasadena, CA
Redondo Beach, CA
(Schedule appointments
through Los Angeles office)
(213) 386–7601

CONSUMER CREDIT
COUNSELORS
TWIN CITIES
729 "D" Street
Marysville, CA 95901
Rodney N. Kennedy,
Executive Director
(916) 743–1785

CONSUMER CREDIT
COUNSELORS
OF EAST BAY (OAKLAND)
1212 Broadway, Suite 706
Oakland, CA 94612
R. F. Happ,
Manager
(415) 832–7555

Branch Offices:
Martinez, CA
Vallejo, CA
(Schedule appointments
through Oakland office)
(415) 832–7555

CALIFORNIA (Continued)

CONSUMER CREDIT COUNSELORS OF THE NORTH VALLEY
1670 Market Street
#18 Downtown Mall
P.O. Box 4044
Redding, CA 96001
Phyllis Solberg,
Manager
(916) 244–9626

CONSUMER CREDIT COUNSELORS OF INLAND EMPIRE
3679 Arlington Avenue, Suite E
Riverside, CA 92506
Anthony Fostier,
Executive Director
(714) 781–0114

CONSUMER CREDIT COUNSELORS OF SACRAMENTO, INC.
1815 "J" Street
Sacramento, CA 95814
Lee A. Sweet,
CCCE, Executive
Vice President/Manager
(916) 444–0740

Branch Office:
Fairfield, CA
(916) 444–0740

CONSUMER CREDIT COUNSELORS OF SAN DIEGO
861 Sixth Avenue, Room 403
P.O. Box 2131
San Diego, CA 92112
Robert R. Osborn,
Executive Director
(619) 234–4118

CONSUMER CREDIT COUNSELORS OF SAN FRANCISCO AND THE PENINSULA
1275 Market Street, Lobby
San Francisco, CA 94103
Kathy Pietruszewski,
Manager
(415) 431–0510

Branch Office:
Santa Rosa, CA
JoAnn Mithchell,
Manager
(707) 527–9221

CONSUMER CREDIT COUNSELORS OF ORANGE COUNTY, INC.
1616 E. Fourth Street, Suite 130
Santa Ana, CA 92701–5189
Carl Lindquist,
President
(714) 547–8281

CALIFORNIA (Continued)

CONSUMER CREDIT
COUNSELORS
OF SANTA CLARA VALLEY, INC.
1825 De La Cruz Boulevard, Suite 8
Santa Clara, CA 95050
Marilynn Thain,
Executive Director
(408) 988–7881

CONSUMER CREDIT
COUNSELORS
OF STOCKTON
1325 N. Center Street, Suite 2
Stockton, CA 95202
Irene Freeman,
Executive Manager
(209) 464–8319

CONSUMER CREDIT
COUNSELORS
OF VENTURA COUNTY
3445 Telegraph Road, Suite 105
Ventura, CA 93003
Marlene Weatherly,
Executive Director
(805) 644–1500

Branch Offices:
San Luis Obispo, CA
Santa Barbara, CA
Thousand Oaks, CA
(Schedule appointments through Ventura Office)
(805) 644–1500

COLORADO

CONSUMER CREDIT
COUNSELING SERVICE
OF GREATER DENVER, INC.
P.O. Box 22557, #1072
5250 Leetsdale Drive
Denver, CO 80222
Larry Smith,
President
(303) 321–8988

CONNECTICUT

CONSUMER CREDIT
COUNSELING SERVICE
OF CONNECTICUT
36 Woodland Streeet
Hartford, CT 06105
Beverly Tuttle,
Executive Director
(203) 247–9517
Branch Offices:
U.S. Submarine Base,
Groton, CT
(203) 449–3383
New Haven, CT
(203) 247–9517

DELAWARE

No Service Reported

DISTRICT OF COLUMBIA

CONSUMER CREDIT
COUNSELING AND
EDUCATIONAL SERVICE OF
GREATER WASHINGTON,
INC.
(Branch Office of CCC & ES,
Rockville, MD)
1120 G Street, N.W. Suite 175B
Washington, D.C. 20005
James Sengstack,
Branch Director
(202) 638–6996

FLORIDA

FAMILY COUNSELING
SERVICE
(CCCS Division)
1639 Atlantic Boulevard, Suite 101
Jacksonville, FL 32207
Richard J. McCulloch,
Executive Director
(904) 396–4846

CONSUMER CREDIT
COUNSELING SERVICE
OF PINELLAS COUNTY, INC.
801 W. Bay Drive, Suite 313
S.E. Bank Building
Largo, FL 33540
Patricia Nurse,
Executive Director
(813) 585–0099

CONSUMER CREDIT
COUNSELING SERVICE
OF SOUTH FLORIDA, INC.
1190 N.E. 125th Street, Suite 11
North Miami, FL 33161
Andrew J. McGehee,
Executive Director
(305) 893–0731

Branch Offices:
Cutler Ridge, FL
Toni Langston,
Manager
(305) 233–2480
Fort Lauderdale, FL
Sue Kahn, Manager
(305) 765–0502

CONSUMER CREDIT
COUNSELING SERVICE
OF CENTRAL FLORIDA, INC.
1900 N. Mills Avenue, #5
Orlando, FL 32803
George C. Reed,
Executive Director
(305) 896–2463

Branch Offices:
Lakeland, FL
(813) 686–6171
Seminole County, FL
Patricia Capsanes,
Manager/Counselor
(305) 339–6111
Volusia County, Florida
Edward Dolne,
Manager/Counselor
(904) 253–0563

FLORIDA (Continued)

CONSUMER CREDIT
COUNSELING SERVICE
OF WEST FLORIDA, INC.
Suite 335, Brent Building
3 West Garden Street
P.O. Box 943
Pensacola, FL 32594
H. Ed Turner,
Treasurer
(904) 434–0268

CONSUMER CREDIT
COUNSELING SERVICE
OF BREVARD
Division of Family
Counseling Center
220 Coral Sands Drive, Suite 1
P.O. Box 63
Rockledge, FL 32955
Robert A. Caldwell, ACSW
Executive Director
Sidney T. Brooks,
Manager
(305) 632–5792

CONSUMER CREDIT
COUNSELING SERVICE
OF THE TAMPA BAY AREA,
INC.
730 S. Sterling Avenue, Suite 300
Mailing Address:
P.O. Box 18835
Tampa, FL 33679–8835
John C. McLaughlin,
President and Chief
Operating Officer
(813) 876–2749

CONSUMER CREDIT
COUNSELING SERVICE
OF PALM BEACH COUNTY,
INC.
224 Datura Street, Suite 205
West Palm Beach, FL 33401
Dorothy G. Kunze,
Executive Director
(305) 655–0885

Branch Offices:
Boca Raton East, FL
(305) 391–2402
Boca Raton West, FL
(305) 482–0269
Port St. Lucie, FL
(305) 878–8000

GEORGIA

CONSUMER CREDIT
COUNSELING SERVICE
OF GREATER ATLANTA, INC.
100 Edgewood Avenue, N.E.
Suite 810
Atlanta, GA 30303
Fred R. Tonney,
President
(404) 659–4391

Branch Office:
Cobb County, GA
James O. Wood, Jr.,
Senior Counselor
(404) 422–5291

GEORGIA (Continued)

CONSUMER CREDIT
COUNSELING SERVICE
OF MIDDLE GEORGIA, INC.
654 First Street, Suite 5
P. O. Box 31
Macon, GA 31202
William P. Boisclair,
Executive Director
(912) 745–6197

CONSUMER CREDIT
COUNSELING SERVICE
OF THE SAVANNAH AREA,
INC.
15 East Montgomery Crossroads
Suites A and B
Savannah, GA 31499
W. Otis Beasley,
Executive Director
(912) 927–HELP

HAWAII

CONSUMER CREDIT
COUNSELING SERVICE
OF HAWAII
1125 N. King Street, Suite 204
Honolulu, HI 96817
Peggy Young,
Director
(808) 841–7516

IDAHO

CONSUMER CREDIT
COUNSELING SERVICE
OF IDAHO, INC.
P.O. Box 9264
6068 Emerald
Boise, ID 83703
B. Jan Brockett,
Executive Director
(208) 375–8140

Branch Offices:
Nampa, ID
(208) 467–2927
Twin Falls, ID
(208) 733–0586

CONSUMER CREDIT
COUNSELING SERVICE
OF NORTHERN IDAHO, INC.
307 Weisburger Building
Lewiston, ID 83501
Lydia Hosmer,
Director
(208) 746–0127

CONSUMER CREDIT
COUNSELING SERVICE
OF SOUTHEASTERN IDAHO,
INC.
P.O. Box 112
343 W. Lewis
Pocatello, ID 83204–0112
Lola Harmison,
Executive Director
(208) 233–7640

ILLINOIS

FAMILY COUNSELING SERVICE
122 W. Downer Place
Aurora, IL 60506
Karl Flodstrom, Director
(312) 844–6820

FAMILY COUNSELING CENTER
201 E. Grove, Suite 200
Bloomington, Illinois 61701
Jo Stephen Major, Executive Director
(309) 828–4343

UNITED CHARITIES OF CHICAGO
14 E. Jackson Boulevard
Chicago, IL 60604
Sue Pape, Director of Family Service
(312) 461–0800

Branch Offices:
Calumet Family Center, IL
(312) 264–3010
Loop Family Center, IL
(312) 939–1300
Parkside Family Center, IL
(312) 282–9535
Family and Mental Health Services of Southwest Cook County, IL
(312) 448–5700

FAMILY SERVICE ASSOCIATION OF GREATER ELGIN AREA
Financial Counseling Service
22 S. Spring Street
Elgin, IL 60120
Catherine M. Williams, Program Director
(312) 695–3680

CENTRAL ILLINOIS CREDIT COUNSELING SERVICE, INC.
505 First National Bank Building
Peoria, IL 61602
James P. Carr, Executive Director
(309) 676–2941

CONSUMER CREDIT COUNSELING SERVICE OF SPRINGFIELD
1021 S. Fourth Street
Springfield, IL 62703
Ron Peters, Director
(217) 523–3621

FAMILY SERVICE ASSOCIATION OF DUPAGE COUNTY—BUDGET COUNSELING/DEBT MANAGEMENT
402 W. Liberty Drive
Wheaton, IL 60187
Ferdinand O. Pauls, Director
(312) 682–1802

ILLINOIS (Continued)

CONSUMER CREDIT
COUNSELING SERVICE
OF McHENRY COUNTY, INC.
P.O. Box 746
Woodstock, IL 60098
Don Price,
Executive Director
(815) 338–5757

INDIANA

CONSUMER CREDIT
COUNSELING SERVICE
OF TRI-STATE, INC.
715 First Avenue, Suite 37
P.O. Box 4783
Evansville, IN 47711
Connie O. Russell,
Executive Director
(812) 422–1108

CONSUMER CREDIT
COUNSELING SERVICE
OF NORTHEASTERN
INDIANA
345 W. Wayne Street
P.O. Box 11403
Fort Wayne, IN 46858
Thomas E. Hufford,
Executive Director
(219) 422–3806

Branch Office:
Warsaw, IN
(Appointments on Tuesdays)
(800) 552–3650 (In Indiana)
(219) 422–3806 (All Others)

CONSUMER CREDIT
COUNSELING SERVICE OF
NORTHWEST INDIANA, INC.
3660 Grant Street, Suite 5
Gary, IN 46408
Barbara L. Bibb,
Executive Director
(219) 980–4800

CONSUMER CREDIT
COUNSELING SERVICE OF
CENTRAL INDIANA, INC.
615 N. Alabama Street
Indianapolis, IN 46204
Clyde Green,
Executive Director
(317) 632–4501

Branch Office:
Muncie, IN
(317) 632–4501
(800) 382–2227 (Indiana Only)

FAMILY & CHILDREN'S
CENTER, INC.
CCCS Division
1411 Lincoln Way West
Mishawaka, IN 46544
Mary Bryant,
Program Manager
(219) 259–5666

IOWA

FINANCIAL MANAGEMENT
SERVICE
(Family Service Agency)
400 Third Avenue, S.E.
Cedar Rapids, IA 52401–1623
Scott Shook,
Executive Director
(319) 398–3574

CONSUMER CREDIT
COUNSELING SERVICE
A.I.D. Center
206 6th Street
Sioux City, IA 51101
Mike Ford, Counselor
(712) 252–1861

KANSAS

CONSUMER CREDIT
COUNSELING
SERVICE, INC.
227 N. Sante Fe, #207
Salina, KS 67401
Ruth Self,
Counselor
(913) 827–6731

TOPEKA HOUSING
INFORMATION CENTER
Consumer Credit Counseling
Services
1195 S.W. Buchanan, Suite 203
Topeka, KS 66604
Karen Hiller,
Executive Director
Roberta Lindburg,
Program Director
(913) 234–0217

KENTUCKY

No Service Reported

LOUISIANA

CONSUMER CREDIT
COUNSELING SERVICE OF
GREATER NEW ORLEANS,
INC.
1539 Jackson Avenue, Room 201
New Orleans, LA 70130
Vern Svendson,
President and
Chief Executive Officer
(504) 529–2396

MAINE

CREDIT COUNSELING CENTERS, INC.
175 Lancaster Street
P.O. Box 1021
Portland, ME 04101
G. D. (Rick) Dobson, Jr.
Executive Director
(207) 774–6278
(800) 882–CCCS

Branch Office:
Bangor, ME
William Gradie, Manager
(800) 882–CCCS

MARYLAND

CONSUMER CREDIT COUNSELING SERVICE OF MARYLAND, INC.
Bradford Federal Building, 2nd Floor
Fayette Street & Luzerne Avenue
Baltimore, MD 21224
Victor L. Boehm, President
(301) 732–3604

Branch Offices:
Bel Air, MD
Matthew A. Keller, Manager
(301) 838–6112
Hagerstown, MD
John Cable, Manager
(301) 733–5810
Laurel, MD
Joan Wolter, Manager
(301) 498–9400
Salisbury, MD
Wayne Ensor, Manager
(301) 742–4422

CONSUMER CREDIT COUNSELING SERVICE OF SOUTHEAST MARYLAND, INC.
9418 Annapolis Road
Lanham, MD 20706
Laurine C. Gibson, Executive Director
(301) 459–8766

Branch Office:
Temple Hills, MD
Joan P. Kelly, Manager
(301) 423–6902

CONSUMER CREDIT COUNSELING AND EDUCATIONAL SERVICE OF GREATER WASHINGTON, INC.
11426 Rockville Pike
Suite 105
Rockville, MD 20852
Joanne Kerstetter, Executive Director
(301) 231–5833

MASSACHUSETTS

CONSUMER CREDIT COUNSELING SERVICE OF EASTERN MASSACHUSETTS, INC.
8 Winter Street, Suite 1210
Boston, MA 02108
Mel R. Stiller,
Executive Director
(617) 426–6644

Branch Offices:
Brockton, MA
(617) 426–6644
Worcester, MA
(617) 795–1444

PIONEER VALLEY CONSUMER CREDIT COUNSELING SERVICE, INC.
293 Bridge Street, Suite 221
P.O. Box 171
Springfield, MA 01101
Robin Walker,
Executive Director
(413) 788–6106

Branch Offices:
Northampton, MA
Southbridge, MA
(Schedule appointments through Springfield office)
(413) 788–6106

MICHIGAN

No Service Reported

MINNESOTA

FAMILY SERVICE OF DULUTH, INC.
600 Ordean Building
424 W. Superior Street
Duluth, MN 55802
Elizabeth George,
Program Coordinator
(218) 726–4826

CONSUMER CREDIT COUNSELING SERVICE OF MINNESOTA, INC.
600 lst Avenue, N., Suite 790
Minneapolis, MN 55403
Wayne B. Wensley,
President
(612) 339–1485

Branch Office:
St. Paul, MN
(612) 293–9197

MISSISSIPPI

No Service Reported

MISSOURI

CONSUMER CREDIT
COUNSELING SERVICE
OF GREATER KANSAS CITY,
INC.
3435 Broadway, Suite 203
Kansas City, MO 64111
Jerry W. Lewis,
Executive Director
(816) 753–0535

CONSUMER CREDIT
COUNSELING SERVICE OF
METROPOLITAN ST. LOUIS,
INC.
3833 Gravois
St. Louis, MO 63116
Virginia M. Nagel,
Executive Vice President
and Director
(314) 773–3660

Branch Office:
St. Charles, MO
Carol Bello, Counselor
(314) 773–3660

SPRINGFIELD AREA FAMILY
DEBT COUNSELORS
950 St. Louis Street
Springfield, MO 65806
Wendell T. Gregory,
Director
(417) 862–5139

MONTANA

CONSUMER CREDIT
COUNSELING SERVICE
OF BILLINGS, MONTANA
2160 Central, Suite #4
Billings, MT 59102
Kathy Ruegamer,
Manager
(406) 656–3172

CONSUMER CREDIT
COUNSELING SERVICE
OF GALLATIN VALLEY, INC.
Martel Financial Center
220 W. Lamme, Suite C
Bozeman, MT 59715
Marsha Brann,
Executive Director
(406) 586–7653 (message only)
(406) 586–2328

CONSUMER CREDIT
COUNSELING SERVICE
OF CASCADE COUNTY
600 6th Street, N.W., #8
P.O. Box 2343 Great Falls,
MT 59403
Duane Delphy,
Manager
(406) 761–8721

NEBRASKA

CONSUMER CREDIT
COUNSELING SERVICE
OF NEBRASKA, INC.
P.O. Box 31002
Omaha, NE 68131
Donald A. Leu, Jr.,
President
(402) 345–3110

Branch Office:
Lincoln, NE
Sheree Atwood,
Manager
(402) 474–6127

NEVADA

CONSUMER CREDIT
COUNSELING SERVICE
OF LAS VEGAS
3305 Spring Mountain Road,
Suite 60
Las Vegas, NV 89102
Melanie Crews,
Executive Secretary
(702) 364–0344

NEW HAMPSHIRE

FAMILY FINANCIAL
COUNSELING SERVICE
Administrative Office
8 Union Street
P.O. Box 676
Concord, NH 03301
Patricia Muzzey,
Executive Director
(603) 224–6593

Branch Offices:
Keene, NH
Laconia, NH
Manchester, NH
Nashua, NH
Peterborough, NH
(Schedule appointments
through Concord office)
(800) 852–3385

NEW JERSEY

CONSUMER CREDIT
COUNSELING SERVICE
OF NEW JERSEY, INC.
76 Mount Kemble Avenue
Morristown, NJ 07960
Mailing Address:
P.O. Box 97C
Convent Station, NJ 07961
Ruth K. Volger,
Executive Director
(201) 267–4324

Branch Office:
Newark, NJ
(201) 267–4324

NEW MEXICO

CONSUMER CREDIT
COUNSELING SERVICE
OF ALBUQUERQUE, INC.
5318 Menaul, N.E.
Albuquerque, NM 87110–3195
Helen Casey,
Executive Director
(505) 884–6601

NEW YORK

CONSUMER CREDIT
COUNSELING SERVICE
OF BUFFALO, INC.
730 Convention Tower
43 Court Street
Buffalo, NY 14202
John Y. Pax,
Executive Director
(716) 854–1710

FAMILY SERVICE
ASSOCIATION OF
NASSAU COUNTY
129 Jackson Street
Hempstead, NY 11550
Lawrence Gumbs,
Director of Family
Financial Counseling
(516) 485–4600

BUDGET & CREDIT
COUNSELING SERVICES,
INC.
44 E. 23rd Street, Suite 304
New York, NY 10010
Luther R. Gatling,
President
(212) 677–3066

CONSUMER CREDIT
COUNSELING SERVICE
OF ROCHESTER, INC.
50 Chestnut Plaza, Suite 410
Rochester, NY 14604
Charles Foster,
Executive Director
(716) 546–3440

CONSUMER CREDIT
COUNSELING SERVICE OF
CENTRAL NEW YORK, INC.
351 S. Warren Street, #304
Syracuse, NY 13202
Sharon Patchett,
Executive Director
(315) 474–6026

Branch Offices:
Binghamton, NY
(607) 722–1251
Cortland, NY
(607) 753–9301
Fulton, NY
(315) 598–3980
Griffis Air Force Base, NY
(315) 330–1110, X3121
Utica, NY
Patricia Manley,
Counselor
(315) 797–5366

NORTH CAROLINA

CONSUMER CREDIT
COUNSELING SERVICE
OF WESTERN NORTH
CAROLINA, INC.
50 S. French Broad
Plateau Building
P.O. Box 2192
Asheville, NC 28802
Lee Dawes,
Executive Director
(704) 255–5166

CONSUMER CREDIT
COUNSELING SERVICE
(A division of United Family
Services)
301 S. Brevard Street
Charlotte, NC 28202
William M. Pickens,
Division Director
(704) 332–4191

Branch Office:
Union County, NC
(704) 283–1539

CONSUMER CREDIT
COUNSELING SERVICE
OF FAYETTEVILLE
118 Gillespie Street
P.O. Box 272
Fayetteville, NC 28302
Kenneth G. Smith,
Executive Director
(919) 323–3192

FAMILY COUNSELING
SERVICE, INC.
OF GASTON COUNTY
318 South Street
Gastonia, NC 28052
Phil DeLuca,
Acting Director
(704) 864–7704

CONSUMER CREDIT
COUNSELING SERVICE
(A division of Family and
Children's Services of Greater
Greensboro, Inc.)
1301 N. Elm Street
Greensboro, NC 27401
M. Edward Roach,
Program Director
(919) 373–1511

CONSUMER CREDIT
COUNSELING SERVICE
#17 Highway 64–70, S.E.
Hickory, NC 28601
Floyd J. Tucker,
Program Director
(704) 322–7161

CONSUMER CREDIT
COUNSELING
(A division of Family Services
of Wake County, Inc.)
3803 Computer Drive, Suite 101A
Raleigh, NC 27609
DeFrancia L. Scott,
Director
(919) 781–9307

NORTH CAROLINA (Continued)

CONSUMER CREDIT
COUNSELING SERVICE
FAMILY SERVICES
2841 Carolina Beach Road
P.O. Box 944
Wilmington, NC 28402
Teresa Morgan, Counselor
(919) 392–7051

CONSUMER CREDIT
COUNSELING SERVICE OF
FORSYTH COUNTY, INC.
440 First Union National
Bank Building
Winston-Salem, NC 27101
Z. Gray Jackson,
Executive Director
(919) 725–1958

NORTH DAKOTA

THE VILLAGE FAMILY
SERVICE CENTER
1721 S. University Drive
Fargo, ND 58103
Mark Carman,
CCC, Director
(701) 235–3328

Branch Offices:
Bismarck, ND
Susan Wefald,
Counselor
(701) 255–3328
Grand Forks, ND
Sig Meier,
Counselor
(701) 746–4584
Minot, ND
Jim Bailey,
Counselor
(701) 852–3328
Williston, ND
Jan Holmen,
Counselor
(800) 732–4475

OHIO

FAMILY SERVICES OF SUMMIT
COUNTY CCCS DIVISION
212 E. Exchange Street
Akron, OH 44304
Robert P. Labbe, ACSW
Executive Director
Sue Lillis,
Director, CCCS
(216) 376–9494
(216) 376–9351—TTY for Deaf

CONSUMER CREDIT
COUNSELING SERVICE
OF STARK COUNTY, INC.
618 Second Street, N.W.
Canton, OH 44703
Suzanne DeHoff,
Executive Director
(216) 455–8118

OHIO
(Continued)

FAMILY CREDIT
COUNSELING SERVICE
(A Division of Family Service
of the Cincinnati Area)
205 West 4th Street
Cincinnati, OH 45202
Bernard Kaiser,
Program Director
(513) 381–6300

CONSUMER CREDIT
COUNSELING SERVICE
OF NORTHEASTERN OHIO
423 Euclid Avenue
Cleveland, OH 44114
William De Vries,
President/Director
(216) 781–8624 (in Cleveland)
(800) 621–8261 (all others)

Branch Offices:
Cuyahoga County, OH
Geauga County, OH
Lake County, OH
Loraine County, OH
(Schedule all appointments
through Cleveland Office)
(800) 621–8261

CONSUMER CREDIT
COUNSELING SERVICE
OF CENTRAL OHIO, INC.
697 Broad Street
Columbus, OH 43215
Paul B. Eberts,
President/Executive
Director
(614) 464–2227

Branch Offices:
Chillicothe, OH
(614) 464–2227
Delaware, OH
(614) 464–2227
Lancaster, OH
(614) 464–2227
Mansfield, OH
(419) 524–0733
Marion, OH
(614) 464–2227

LUTHERAN SOCIAL SERVICES
CCCS Department
P.O. Box 506
3304 N. Main Street
Dayton, OH 45405
Robert F. Libecap,
Program Manager
(513) 278–9617
Branch Office:
Sidney, OH
(513) 492–1953

CONSUMER CREDIT
COUNSELING SERVICE
FAMILY SERVICE OF
BUTLER COUNTY
111 Buckeye Street
Hamilton, OH 45011
Irma Sandage,
Executive Director
(513) 868–9220

CONSUMER CREDIT
COUNSELING SERVICE
OF PORTAGE COUNTY
302 North Depeyster
Kent, OH 44240
Mary Sites,
Coordinator
(216) 678–4782

OHIO
(Continued)

CONSUMER CREDIT
COUNSELING SERVICE
OF COLUMBIANA COUNTY
964 N. Market Street
P.O. Box 413
Lisbon, OH 44432
John A. Hudak,
Executive Director
(216) 424–9509

CONSUMER CREDIT
COUNSELING SERVICE
FAMILY COUNSELING
SERVICE
126 W. Church Street
Newark, OH 43055
Dorothy Higgins,
Program Manager
(614) 349–7051

Branch Office:
Mt. Vernon, OH
(614) 349–7066

CHILDREN'S AND FAMILY
SERVICE ASSOCIATION
CCCS OF THE UPPER OHIO
VALLEY

(Branch of Children's and
Family Service Association,
Wheeling, West Virginia)
Steubenville, OH
Lonnie Williams,
Executive Vice President
(614) 283–4763

CONSUMER CREDIT
COUNSELING PROGRAM
1704 North Road, S.E.
Heaton Square
Warren, OH 44484
Nancy Gray,
Coordinator
(216) 856–2907

CHILDREN'S & FAMILY
SERVICE CCCS DIVISION
535 Marmion Avenue
Youngstown, OH 44502
Kathy Virgallito,
Program Director
(216) 782–5664

CONSUMER CREDIT
COUNSELING SERVICE
OF MUSKINGUM VALLEY
721 Market Street
Zanesville, OH 43701
Rebecca Donne,
Executive Director
Rebecca Bee,
Program Manager
(614) 454–6872

Branch Office:
New Lexington, OH
(614) 342–1063

OKLAHOMA

CONSUMER CREDIT
COUNSELING SERVICE
OF CENTRAL OKLAHOMA,
INC.
2519 Northwest 23rd
P.O. Box 75405
Oklahoma City, OK 73147
Gloria E. Kelley,
Executive Director
(405) 947–6631

CREDIT COUNSELING
CENTERS OF OKLAHOMA,
INC.
2140 South Harvard
P.O. Box 4450
Tulsa, OK 74159
Victor R. Schock,
Director
(918) 744–5611

OREGON

CONSUMER CREDIT
COUNSELING SERVICE
OF LINN-BENTON, INC.
201 West First
P.O. Box 1006
Albany, OR 97321
Jan Amling,
Executive Director
(503) 926–5843

CONSUMER CREDIT
COUNSELING SERVICE OF
CENTRAL OREGON, INC.
2115 N.E. Division, Suite A
Bend, OR 97701–3599
Dee Foss,
Executive Director
(503) 389–6181

CONSUMER CREDIT
COUNSELING SERVICE
OF LANE COUNTY, INC.
1601—B, Oak Street
Eugene, OR 97401
Evelyn L. Smith,
Executive Director
(503) 342–4459

CONSUMER CREDIT
COUNSELING SERVICE OF
SOUTHERN OREGON, INC.
33 N. Central, #300
Medford, OR 97501
Jan Safely,
Office Manager
(503) 779–2273

Branch Office:
Klamath Falls, OR
(503) 884–5193

COOS-CURRY CONSUMER
CREDIT COUNSELING
SERVICE
Pony Village Mall
North Bend, OR 97459
Deborah L. Graham,
Executive Director
(503) 756–4008

OREGON
(Continued)

CONSUMER CREDIT
COUNSELING SERVICE
OF OREGON, INC.
3420 S.E. Powell Boulevard
P.O. Box 42155
Portland, OR 97242
Lawrence Winthrop,
President
(503) 232–8139

DOUGLAS CONSUMER CREDIT
COUNSELING SERVICE
P.O. Box 1011
Roseburg, OR 97470
Jan Phelps,
Executive Director
(503) 673–3104

CONSUMER CREDIT
COUNSELING SERVICE
OF MID-WILLIAMETTE
VALLEY, INC.
665 Cottage, N.E.
Salem, OR 97301
Frank Lackey,
Executive Director
(503) 581–7301

PENNSYLVANIA

CONSUMER CREDIT
COUNSELING SERVICE OF
LEHIGH VALLEY, INC.
1031 Linden Street
Allentown, PA 18102
Albert J. Kotch,
Executive Director
(215) 821–4011

Branch Office:
Reading, PA
Slate Belt Medical Center, PA
(Schedule appointments
through Allentown Office)
(215) 821–4011

CONSUMER CREDIT
COUNSELING DIVISION
FAMILY SERVICES
110 W. 10th Street, Room 208
Erie, PA 16501
David C. Shiel, ACSW
(814) 454–6478

CONSUMER CREDIT
COUNSELING SERVICE
OF DELAWARE VALLEY
(Also serving southern New
Jersey and Delaware)
1211 Chestnut Street, Suite 411
Philadelphia, PA 19107
Thomas A. O'Neill,
Executive Director
(215) 563–5665 or 563–5694

Branch Office:
West Chester, PA
(215) 563–5665

CONSUMER CREDIT
COUNSELING SERVICE OF
WESTERN PENNSYLVANIA,
INC.
309 Smithfield Street, Suite 5000
Pittsburgh, PA 15222
Carl J. Eidenmuller,
President
(412) 471–7584

PENNSYLVANIA (Continued)

Branch Offices:
Blair County, PA
Diane Karikas,
Counselor
(814) 696–3546
Greensburg, PA
Edward Graszl,
Counselor
(412) 838–1290
New Castle, PA
Mary Ellen Sotus,
Counselor
(412) 652–8074

CONSUMER CREDIT
COUNSELING SERVICE
OF NORTHEASTERN
PENNSYLVANIA, INC.
402 Connell Building
P.O. Box 168
Scranton, PA 18501
Michael A. Elick,
Executive Director
(717) 342–1072 or 655–9527

RHODE ISLAND

CONSUMER CREDIT
COUNSELING DIVISION
RHODE ISLAND
CONSUMERS' COUNCIL
365 Broadway
Providence, RI 02909
Paul F. McHale,
Administrator
(401) 277–2764

SOUTH CAROLINA

CONSUMER CREDIT
COUNSELING SERVICE
OF GREATER CHARLESTON,
S.C.
3005 W. Montague, Suite C
Charleston, SC 29418
Donald Buckland,
Director
(803) 747–3616

FAMILY SERVICE CENTER
1800 Main Street
P.O. Box 7876
Columbia, SC 29202
L. Russell Rawls, Jr.,
Executive Director
M. Susie Irvine,
Coordinator, CCCS
(803) 733–5450

Branch Office:
ACS Fort Jackson, SC
William M. Meares,
Counselor
(803) 751–5256

FAMILY SERVICE
GREENVILLE
844 E. Washington Street
P.O. Box 10306, Federal Station
Greenville, SC 29603
Amelia K. Croft, ACSW
Executive Director
(803) 232–2434 or 232–6266

SOUTH DAKOTA

CONSUMER CREDIT
COUNSELING SERVICE
OF THE BLACK HILLS
P.O. Box 14
7th and Kansas City Streets
Rapid City, SD 57709
Flo A. Brenton,
Director
(605) 348–4550

LUTHERAN SOCIAL
SERVICES OF SOUTH
DAKOTA
CCCS Division
600 W. 12th Street
Sioux Falls, SD 57104
Judy Reinke,
Program Director
(605) 336–3387

TENNESSEE

FAMILY & CHILDREN'S
SERVICES OF
CHATTANOOGA
CCCS Division
323 High Street
Chattanooga, TN 37403
Sharon Cabeen,
Supervisor
(615) 755–2860

CONSUMER CREDIT
COUNSELING SERVICE OF
GREATER KNOXVILLE, INC.
Suite 200, 705 Broadway
P.O. Box 3343
Knoxville, TN 37927–3343
Sue L. Brown,
Director
(615) 522–2661 or 522–7151

CONSUMER CREDIT
COUNSELING SERVICE OF
METROPOLITAN
NASHVILLE, INC.
250 Venture Circle, Suite 205
Nashville, TN 37228–1604
Marvin N. Wright,
Executive Director
(615) 244–5184 or 244–5185

TEXAS

CHILD AND FAMILY SERVICE
CCCS Division
2001 Chicon Street
Austin, TX 78722
Bob Bowman,
Executive Director
Lonnie Williams,
CCCS Division Director
(512) 478–1648

MONEY MANAGEMENT
COUNSELING & SERVICES
1721 S. Brownlee Boulevard
Corpus Christi, TX 78404
David C. Melton,
Executive Director
(512) 882–1791

TEXAS
(Continued)

CONSUMER CREDIT
COUNSELING SERVICE OF
GREATER DALLAS, INC.
5415 Maple Avenue, Suite 205
Dallas, TX 75235–7490
David H. Dugan,
Executive Director
(214) 634–1560

Branch Office:
Richardson, TX
Nancy Fernandez,
Counselor
(214) 437–6252

CONSUMER CREDIT
COUNSELING SERVICE
Y.W.C.A.
1600 N. Brown Street
El Paso, TX 79902
Darlene Gade,
Executive Director
(915) 533–7475 X42

CONSUMER CREDIT
COUNSELING SERVICE
OF GREATER FORT WORTH,
INC.
807 Texas Street, Suite 104
Fort Worth, TX 76102
Warren E. Coggins,
Executive Director
(817) 334–0151

CONSUMER CREDIT
COUNSELING SERVICE OF
HOUSTON AND THE GULF
COAST AREA, INC.
4203 Fannin Street
Houston, TX 77004
Terry M. Blaney,
President
(713) 520–0742

Branch Offices:
Fannin, TX
Jean Law,
Director
(713) 520–0742
Fort Bend County, TX
Bayla Abrams,
Director
(713) 520–0742 or 499–5681
Montgomery County, TX
Louise Rochford,
Director
(713) 520–0742 or 363–4364
Pasadena, TX
Nancy Koretz,
Director
(713) 520–0742

CONSUMER CREDIT
COUNSELING OF NORTH
CENTRAL TEXAS, INC.
1006 W. University Drive
McKinney, TX 75069
Pamela Gray,
Executive Director
(214) 542–0257

Branch Offices:
Denton, TX
(817) 382–0331
Greenville, TX
(214) 455–3987
Plano, TX
(214) 542–0257
Sherman, TX
(214) 892–6927

TEXAS (Continued)

CONSUMER CREDIT COUNSELING SERVICE OF GREATER SAN ANTONIO, INC.
4203 Woodcock, Suite 251
San Antonio, TX 78228
Ruby Bainum,
Director
(512) 734–8112

UTAH

COMMUNITY CONSUMER CREDIT COUNSELING SERVICE OF NORTHERN UTAH, INC.
295 30th Street, P.O. Box 547
Ogden, UT 84402
Brent Littlefield,
President
(801) 394–7759

CONSUMER CREDIT COUNSELING SERVICE OF UTAH, INC.
220 E. 3900 South, Suite 1
Salt Lake City, UT 84107
Dale G. Taylor,
Executive Director
(801) 266–0064

VERMONT

FAMILY FINANCIAL COUNSELING SERVICE (BRATTLEBORO, VT)
(Branch of FFCS, Concord, NH)
(603) 244–6593, call collect

FAMILY FINANCIAL COUNSELING SERVICE (BENNINGTON, VT)
(Branch of FFCS, Concord, NH)
(603) 224–6593, call collect

VIRGINIA

CONSUMER CREDIT COUNSELING AND EDUCATIONAL SERVICE OF NORTHERN VIRGINIA
(Branch of CCC & ES OF GREATER WASHINGTON)
300 Montgomery Street
Alexandria, VA 22314
Marilyn Morgan,
Branch Director
(703) 836–8772

CONSUMER CREDIT COUNSELING AND EDUCATIONAL SERVICE OF NORTHERN VIRGINIA
(Branch of CCC & ES OF GREATER WASHINGTON)
3541 Chain Bridge Road, Suite 3A
Fairfax, VA 22030
Judy McCoid,
Branch Director
(703) 591–9020

VIRGINIA (Continued)

PENINSULA FAMILY SERVICE
AND TRAVELLERS AID, INC.
CCCS Division
1520 Aberdeen Road
P.O. Box 7315
Hampton, VA 23666
Edwin Cotten,
Executive Director
(804) 827–8344

Branch Office:
Williamsburg, VA
Edwin Cotten,
Executive Director
(804) 874–6580

CONSUMER CREDIT
COUNSELING SERVICE
OF TIDEWATER
(Division of Family Services)
222 Nineteenth Street West
Norfolk, VA 23517
Sharon Brooks,
Program Coordinator
(804) 622–7017

CONSUMER CREDIT
COUNSELING SERVICE
OF VIRGINIA, INC.
6 N. Sixth Street, Suite 200
Richmond, VA 23219
Robert E. Bryan,
Executive Director
(804) 780–9042

Branch Offices:
Fredericksburg, VA
Dale Leite,
Manager
(703) 371–7575

Petersburg, VA
Vicki Lynn,
Manager
(804) 862–4300

CONSUMER CREDIT
COUNSELING SERVICE OF
ROANOKE VALLEY, INC.
104 W. Campbell Ave.
State and City Building, Suite 703
Roanoke, VA 24011
Virginia H. Gayle,
Executive Director
(703) 342–3724

WASHINGTON

CONSUMER CREDIT
COUNSELING SERVICE
OF THE TRI-CITIES
113 W. Kennewick Avenue
P.O. Box 6551
Kennewick, WA 99336
Thelma Flanagan,
Executive Director
(509) 586–2181

CONSUMER CREDIT
COUNSELING SERVICE
OF SEATTLE
2326 Sixth Avenue, Suite 206
Seattle, WA 98121
S. F. Williams,
President
(206) 441–3291

WASHINGTON (Continued)

Branch Offices:
Everett, WA
(206) 441–3291
Naval Air Station/Whidby Island
Betty Justus, Counselor/Area Representative
(206) 679–2545
Oak Harbor, WA
(204) 679–5076

CONSUMER CREDIT COUNSELING SERVICE OF TACOMA-PIERCE
11300 Bridgeport Way, S.W.
Suite D
Tacoma, WA 98499
Laura G. Johnson, Executive Director
(206) 588–1858

CONSUMER CREDIT COUNSELING SERVICE OF YAKIMA VALLEY
1218 W. Lincoln
Yakima, WA 98902
Georgia W. Norcott, Executive Director
(509) 248–5270

WEST VIRGINIA

CONSUMER CREDIT COUNSELING SERVICE OF SOUTHERN WEST VIRGINIA, INC.
Room A–117, Pinecrest Office Complex
P.O. Box 2129
Beckley, WV 25802
Raymond L. Coleman, Executive Director
(304) 255–2499

CONSUMER CREDIT COUNSELING SERVICE OF THE KANAWHA VALLEY
503 Terminal Building
8 Capitol Street
Charleston, WV 25301
Geraldine Allen, Manager
(304) 344–3843

CONSUMER CREDIT COUNSELING SERVICE OF NORTH CENTRAL WEST VIRGINIA CRISS-CROSS, INC.
166 Washington Avenue
P.O. Box 1831
Clarksburg, WV 26302–1831
Edward J. Welp, MSW, Executive Director
(304) 623–0921

WEST VIRGINIA (Continued)

CONSUMER CREDIT COUNSELING OF FAMILY SERVICE, INC.
1007 Fifth Avenue
Huntington, WV 25701
Jane M. Chafin,
Executive Director
(304) 522–4321

CONSUMER CREDIT COUNSELING SERVICE OF THE MID-OHIO VALLEY, INC.
4101/2 Market Street
P.O. Box 454
Parkersburg, WV 26102
June Shelene,
Manager
(304) 485–3141 or 485–6280

CHILDREN AND FAMILY SERVICE ASSOCIATION CCCS OF THE UPPER OHIO VALLEY
51 11th Street
Wheeling, WV 26003
Lonnie Wineman,
Executive
Vice President
(304) 232–6733

Branch Office:
CHILDREN AND FAMILY SERVICE ASSOCIATION
(Steubenville, OH)
Lonnie Wineman,
Executive
Vice President
(614) 283–4763

WISCONSIN

No Service Reported

WYOMING

No Service Reported

CANADIAN AGENCIES

Affiliated with the National Foundation for Consumer Credit

CREDIT COUNSELLING SERVICE OF METROPOLITAN TORONTO
100 Lombard Street, Suite 301
Toronto, Ontario M5C 1M3
Beulam "Sam" Hastings
Executive Director
(416) 366–5251

For further information on Canadian counseling locations contact:

THE ONTARIO ASSOCIATION OF CREDIT COUNSELLING SERVICES
297 Lakeshore Road, East, Suite 5
P.O. Box 248
Oakville, Ontario,
Canada L6J 5A2
Ronald M. Mason,
Executive Director
(416) 845 2423

FAIR CREDIT REPORTING ACT

FAIR CREDIT REPORTING ACT

APPENDIX 153–A

Synopsis

Sec.

602 Findings and purpose
603 Definitions and rules of construction
604 Permissible purposes of reports
605 Obsolete information
606 Disclosure of investigative consumer reports
607 Compliance procedures
608 Disclosures to governmental agencies
609 Disclosures to consumers
610 Conditions of disclosure to consumers
611 Procedure in case of disputed accuracy
612 Charges for certain disclosures
613 Public record information for employment purposes
614 Restrictions on investigative consumer reports
615 Requirements on users of consumer reports
616 Civil liability for willful noncompliance
617 Civil liability for negligent noncompliance
618 Jurisdiction of courts; limitation of actions
619 Obtaining information under false pretenses
620 Unauthorized disclosures by officers or employees
621 Administrative enforcement
622 Relation to State laws

FAIR CREDIT REPORTING ACT

The Fair Credit Reporting Act (FCRA) covers all reporting on individuals as consumers, whether in connections with obtaining credit, insurance, or employment. Credit or other reports on business firms, or the business activities of individuals, are specifically excluded from the coverage of the act.

The FCRA creates the following consumer rights:

(1) To be told the reasons for adverse action on an application for credit, insurance, or employment when a credit report was a factor, and to be given the name and address of the credit reporting agency.

(2) To be informed of the nature and substance of all information in one's credit file by the credit reporting agency.

(3) To have another person present at the credit reporting agency when one's credit file is discussed.

(4) To be told who has received credit reports during the preceding six months for credit or insurance purposes, and during the preceding two years for employment purposes.

(5) To have inaccurate or unverifiable information deleted from the file.

(6) To have the information in the file reinvestigated whenever its accuracy is disputed.

(7) To have the right to file a brief explanatory statement in connection with disputed items, and to have that statement included in subsequent reports.

(8) To have the information in the file kept confidential and used only for legitimate business purposes.

(9) To have personal information in the file kept

from governmental agencies unless otherwise ordered by a court.

(10) To be informed when adverse public record information is reported for employment purposes, or to have this information kept current.

(11) To have adverse information deleted from the file after seven years, or after ten years in the case of bankruptcy.

(12) To be informed of the scope and nature of investigative reports on one's personal life.

(13) To have adverse information contained in investigative reports reverified before it can be used again.

(14) To collect actual damages in civil actions against negligent credit reporting agencies, and punitive damages where the agency was willful in reporting inaccurate information.

Requirements for Consumer Reporting Agencies

Consumer reporting agency may furnish consumer reports only for permissible purposes including use in credit extensions or reviews and collections of accounts as well as responses to court orders or written consumer instructions; credit information must be current and accurate, and consumer can obtain contents of his file; agency must reinvestigate if information challenged, and disclose consumer's assertions if consumer supplies them; adverse information in investigative consumer reports must be reinvestigated every three months; government agencies can obtain only identifying information if request not for permissible purpose.

[I] Permissible Purpose

A consumer reporting agency may furnish consumer reports only for prescribed reasons, referred to as "permissible purposes." These purposes are

(1) in response to an order of a court having jurisdiction to issue the order;

(2) in response to written instructions from the consumer to whom the report relates;

(3) for use by a person in connection with a credit transaction and involving the extension of credit to, or review or collection of an account of, the consumer to whom the report relates;

(4) for use by a person in connection with an employment decision;

(5) for use by a person in determining a consumer's eligibility for a license or other benefit granted by a governmental instrumentality required by law to consider an applicant's financial responsibility or status; and

(6) for use by a person with a legitimate business need for the information in connection with a business transaction involving the consumer.

§ 602 Findings and purpose

(a) The Congress makes the following findings:

(1) The banking system is dependent upon fair and accurate credit reporting. Inaccurate credit reports directly impair the efficiency of the banking system, and unfair credit reporting methods undermine the public confidence which is essential to the continued functioning of the banking system.

(2) An elaborate mechanism has been developed for investigating and evaluating the credit worthiness, credit standing, credit capacity, character, and general reputation of consumers.

(3) Consumer reporting agencies have assumed a vital role in assembling and evaluating consumer credit and other information on consumers.

(4) There is a need to insure that consumer reporting agencies exercise their grave responsibilities with fairness, impartiality, and a respect for the consumer's right of privacy.

(b) It is the purpose of this title to require that consumer reporting agencies adopt reasonable procedures for meeting the needs of commerce for consumer credit, personnel, insurance, and other information in a manner which is fair and equitable to the consumer, with regard to the confidentiality, accuracy, relevancy, and proper utilization of such information in accordance with the requirements of this title.

[15 U.S.C. 1681. Pub. L. 90–321, 602, as added by Act of Oct. 26, 1970, Pub. L. 91–508, 601, 84 Stat. 1128.]

§ 603 Definitions and rules of construction

(a) Definitions and rules of construction set forth in this section are applicable for the purposes of this title.

(b) The term "person" means any individual, partnership, corporation, trust, estate, cooperative, association, government or governmental subdivision or agency, or other entity.

(c) The term "consumer" means an individual.

(d) The term "consumer report" means any written, oral, or other communication of any information by a consumer reporting agency bearing on a consumer's credit worthiness, credit standing, credit capacity, character, general reputation, personal characteristics, or mode of living which is used or expected to be used or collected in whole or in part for the purpose of serving as a factor in establishing the consumer's eligibility for (1) credit or insurance to be used primarily for personal, family, or household purposes, or (2) employment purposes, or (3) other purposes authorized under section 1681b of this title. The term does not include (A) any report containing information solely as to transactions or experiences between the consumer and the person making the report; (B) any authorization or approval of a specific extension of credit directly or indirectly by the issuer of a credit card or similar device; or (C) any report in which a person who has been requested by a third party to make a specific extension of credit directly or indirectly to a consumer conveys his decision with respect to such request, if the third party advises the consumer of the name and address of the person to whom the request was made and such person makes the disclosures to the consumer required under section 1681m of this title.

(e) The term "investigative consumer report" means a consumer report or portion thereof in which information on a consumer's character, general reputation, personal characteristics, or mode of living is obtained through personal interviews with neighbors, friends, or associates of the consumer reported on or with others with whom he is acquainted or who may have knowledge concerning any such items of information. However, such information shall not include specific factual information on a consumer's credit record obtained directly from a creditor of the consumer or from a consumer reporting agency when such information was obtained directly from a creditor of the consumer or from the consumer.

(f) The term "consumer reporting agency" means any person which, for monetary fees, dues, or on a cooperative nonprofit basis, regularly engages in whole or in part in the practice of assembling or evaluating consumer credit information or other information on consumers for the purpose of furnishing consumer reports to third parties, and which uses any means or facility of interstate commerce for the purpose of preparing or furnishing consumer reports.

(g) The term "file," when used in connection with information on any consumer, means all of the information on that consumer recorded and retained by a consumer reporting agency regardless of how the information is stored.

(h) The term "employment purposes" when used in connection with a consumer report means a report used for the purpose of evaluating a consumer for employment, promotion, reassignment or retention as an employee.

(i) The term "medical information" means information or records obtained, with the consent of the individual to whom it relates, from licensed physicians or medical practitioners, hospitals, clinics, or other medical or medically related facilities.

[15 U.S.C. 1681a. Pub. L. 90–321, 603, as added by Act of Oct. 26, 1970, Pub. L. 91–508, 601, 84 Stat. 1128.]

§ 604 Permissible purpose of reports.

A consumer reporting agency may furnish a consumer report under the following circumstances and no other:

(1) In response to the order of a court having jurisdiction to issue such an order.

(2) In accordance with the written instructions of the consumer to whom it relates.

(3) To a person which it has reason to believe

(A) intends to use the information in connection with a credit transaction involving the consumer on whom the information is to be furnished and involving the extension of credit to, or review or collection of an account of, the consumer; or

(B) intends to use the information for employment purposes; or

(C) intends to use the information in connection with the underwriting of insurance involving the consumer; or

(D) intends to use the information in connection with a determination of the consumer's eligibility for a license or other benefit granted by a governmental instrumentality required by law to consider an applicant's financial responsibility or status; or

(E) otherwise has a legitimate business need for the information in connection with a business transaction involving the consumer.

[15 U.S.C. 1681b. Pub. L. 90–321, 604, as added by Act of Oct. 26, 1970, Pub. L. 91–508, 601, 84 Stat. 1129.]

§ 605 Obsolete information

(a) Except as authorized under subsection (b), no consumer reporting agency may make any consumer report containing any of the following items of information.

(1) Bankruptcies which, from date of adjudication of most recent bankruptcy, antedate the report by more than ten years.

(2) Suits and judgments which, from date of entry, antedate the report by more than seven years or until the governing statute of limitations has expired, whichever is the longer period.

(3) Paid tax liens which, from day of payment, antedate the report by more than seven years.

(4) Accounts placed for collection or charged to profit and loss which antedate the report by more than seven years.

(5) Records of arrest, indictment, or conviction of crime which, from date of disposition, release, or parole, antedate the report by more than seven years.

(6) Any other adverse item of information which antedates the report by more than seven years.

(b) The provisions of subsection (a) are not applicable in the case of any consumer credit report to be used in connection with:

(1) a credit transaction involving, or which may reasonably be expected to involve, a principal amount of $50,000 or more;

(2) the underwriting of life insurance involving, or which may reasonably be expected to involve, a face amount of $50,000 or more; or

(3) the employment of any individual at an annual salary which equals, or which may reasonably be expected to equal $20,000, or more.

[15 U.S.C. 1681c. Pub. L. 90–321, 605, as added by Act of Oct. 26, 1970, Pub. L. 91–508, 601, 84 Stat. 1129. Amended by Act of Nov. 6, 1978, Pub. L. 95–598, 312(b), 92 Stat. 2676.]

§ 606 Disclosure of investigative consumer reports

(a) A person may not procure or cause to be prepared an investigative consumer report on any consumer unless:

(1) it is clearly and accurately disclosed to the consumer that an investigative consumer report including information as to his character, general reputation, personal characteristics, and mode of living, whichever are applicable, may be made, and such disclosure (A) is made in a writing mailed, or otherwise delivered, to the consumer, not later than three days after the date on which the report was first requested, and (B) includes a statement informing the consumer of his right to request the additional disclosures provided for under subsection (b) of this section; or

(2) the report is to be used for employment purposes for which the consumer has not specifically applied.

(b) Any person who procures or causes to be prepared an investigative consumer report on any consumer shall, upon written request made by the consumer within a reasonable period of time after the receipt by him of the disclosure required by subsection (a)(1), make a complete and accurate disclosure of the nature and scope of the investigation requested. This disclosure shall be made in a writing mailed, or otherwise delivered, to the consumer not later than five days after the date on which the request for such disclosure was received from the consumer or such report was first requested, whichever is the later.

(c) No person may be held liable for any violation of subsection (a) or (b) of this section if he shows by a preponderance of the evidence that at the time of the violation he maintained reasonable procedures to assure compliance with subsection (a) or (b).

[15 U.S.C. 1681d. Pub. L. 90–321, 606, as added by Act of Oct. 26, 1970, Pub. L. 91–508, 601, 84 Stat. 1130.]

§ 607 Compliance procedures

(a) Every consumer reporting agency shall maintain reasonable procedures designed to avoid violations of section 1681c of this title and to limit the furnishing of consumer reports to the purposes listed under section 1681b of this title. These procedures shall require that prospective users of the information identify themselves, certify the purposes for which the information is sought, and certify that the information will be used for no other purpose. Every consumer reporting agency shall make a reasonable effort to verify the identity of a new prospective user and the uses certified by such prospective user prior to furnishing such user a consumer report. No consumer reporting agency may furnish a consumer report to any person if it has reasonable grounds for believing that the consumer report will not be used for a purpose listed in section 1681b of this title.

(b) Whenever a consumer reporting agency prepares a consumer report it shall follow reasonable procedures to assure maximum possible accuracy of the information concerning the individual about whom the report relates.

[15 U.S.C. 1681e. Pub. L. 90–321, 607, as added by Act of Oct. 26, 1970, Pub. L. 91–508, 601, 84 Stat. 1130.]

§ 608 Disclosures to governmental agencies

Notwithstanding the provisions of section 1681b of this title, a consumer reporting agency may furnish identifying information re-specting any consumer, limited to his name, address, former addresses, places of employment, or former places of employment, to a governmental agency.

[15 U.S.C. A 1681f. Pub. L. 90–321, 608, as added by Act of Oct. 26, 1970, Pub. L. 91–508, 601, 84 Stat. 1131.]

§ 609 Disclosures to consumers

(a) Every consumer reporting agency shall, upon request and proper identification of any consumer, clearly and accurately disclose to the consumer:

(1) The nature and substance of all information (except medical information) in its files on the consumer at the time of the request.

(2) The sources of the information; except that the sources of information acquired solely for use in

preparing an investigative consumer report and actually used for no other purpose need not be disclosed: Provided, that in the event an action is brought under this title, such sources shall be available to the plaintiff under appropriate discovery procedures in the court in which the action is brought.

(3) The recipients of any consumer report on the consumer which it has furnished:

(A) for employment purposes within the two-year period preceding the request, and

(B) for any other purpose within the six-month period preceding the request.

(b) The requirements of subsection (a) respecting the disclosure of sources of information and the recipients of consumer reports do not apply to information received or consumer reports furnished prior to the effective date of this title except to the extent that the matter involved is contained in the files of the consumer reporting agency on that date.

[15 U.S.C. 1681g. Pub. L. 90–321, 609, as added by Act of Oct. 26, 1970, Pub. L. 91–508, 601, 84 Stat. 1131.]

§ 610 Conditions of disclosure to consumers

(a) A consumer reporting agency shall make the disclosures required under section 1681g of this title during normal business hours and on reasonable notice.

(b) The disclosures required under section 1681g of this title shall be made to the consumer:

(1) in person if he appears in person and furnishes proper identification; or

(2) by telephone if he has made a written request, with proper identification, for telephone disclosure and the toll charge, if any, for the telephone call is prepaid by or charged directly to the consumer.

(c) Any consumer reporting agency shall provide trained personnel to explain to the consumer any information furnished to him pursuant to section 1681g of this title.

(d) The consumer shall be permitted to be accompanied by one other person of his choosing, who shall furnish reasonable identification. A consumer reporting agency may require the consumer to furnish a written statement granting permission to the consumer reporting agency to discuss the consumer's file in such person's presence.

(e) Except as provided in sections 1681o and 1681p of this title, no consumer may bring any action or proceeding in the nature of defamation, invasion of privacy, or negligence with respect to the reporting of information against any consumer reporting agency, any user of information, or any person who furnishes information to a consumer reporting agency, based on information disclosed pursuant to section 1681g, 1681h, 1681m of this title, except as to false information furnished with malice or willful intent to injure such consumer.

[15 U.S.C. 1681h. Pub. L. 90–321, 610, as added by Act of Oct. 26, 1970, Pub. L. 91–508, 601, 84 Stat. 1131.]

§ 611 Procedure in case of disputed accuracy

(a) If the completeness or accuracy of any item of information contained in his file is disputed by a consumer, and such dispute is directly conveyed to the consumer reporting agency by the consumer, the consumer reporting agency shall within a reasonable period of time reinvestigate and record the current status of that information unless it has reasonable grounds to believe that the dispute by the consumer is frivolous or irrelevant. If after such reinvestigation such information is found to be inaccurate or can no longer be verified, the consumer reporting agency shall promptly delete such information. The presence of contradictory information in the consumer's file does not in and of itself constitute reasonable grounds for believing the dispute is frivolous or irrelevant.

(b) If the reinvestigation does not resolve the dispute, the consumer may file a brief statement setting forth the nature of the dispute. The consumer reporting agency may limit such statements to not more than one hundred words if it provides the consumer with assistance in writing a clear summary of the dispute.

(c) Whenever a statement of a dispute is filed, unless there is reasonable grounds to believe that it is frivolous or irrelevant, the consumer reporting agency shall, in any subsequent consumer report containing the information in question, clearly note that it is disputed by the consumer and provide either the consumer's statement or a clear and accurate codification or summary thereof.

(d) Following any deletion of information which is found to be inaccurate or whose accuracy can no longer be verified or any notation as to disputed information, the consumer reporting agency shall, at the request of the consumer, furnish notification that the item has been deleted or the statement, codification or summary pursuant to subsection (b) or (c) to any person specifically designated by the consumer who has within two years prior thereto received a consumer report for employment purposes, or within six months prior thereto received a consumer report for any other purpose, which contained the deleted or disputed information. The consumer reporting agency shall clearly and conspicuously disclose to the consumer his rights to make such a request. Such disclosure shall be made at or prior to the time the information is deleted or the consumer's statement regarding the disputed information is received.

[15 U.S.C. 1681i. Pub. L. 90–321, 611, as added by Act of Oct. 26, 1970, Pub. L. 91–508, 601, 84 Stat. 1132.]

§ 612 Charges for certain disclosures

A consumer reporting agency shall make all disclosures pursuant to section 1681g of this title and furnish all consumer reports pursuant to section 1681i(d) of this title without charge to the consumer if within thirty days after receipt by such consumer of a notification pursuant to section 1681m of this title or notification from a debt collection agency affiliated with such consumer reporting agency stating that the consumer's credit rating may be or has been adversely affected, the consumer makes a request under section 1681g or

1681i(d) of this title. Otherwise, the consumer reporting agency may impose a reasonable charge on the consumer for making disclosure to such consumer pursuant to section 1681g of this title, the charge for which shall be indicated to the consumer prior to making disclosure; and for furnishing notifications, statements, summaries, or codifications to persons designated by the consumer pursuant to section 1681i(d) of this title, the charge for which shall be indicated to the consumer prior to furnishing such information and shall not exceed the charge that the consumer reporting agency would impose on each designated recipient for a consumer report except that no charge may be made for notifying such persons of the deletion of information which is found to be inaccurate or which can no longer be verified.

[15 U.S.C. 1681j. Pub. L. 90–321, 612, as added by Act of Oct. 26, 1970, Pub. L. 91–508, 601, 84 Stat. 1132.]

§ 613 Public record information for employment purposes

A consumer reporting agency which furnishes a consumer report for employment purposes and which for that purpose compiles and reports items of information on consumers which are matters of public record and are likely to have an adverse effect upon a consumer's ability to obtain employment shall:

(1) at the time such public record information is reported to the user of such consumer report, notify the consumer of the fact that public record information is being reported by the consumer reporting agency, together with the name and address of the person to whom such information is being reported; or

(2) maintain strict procedures designed to insure that whenever public record information which is likely to have an adverse effect on a consumer's ability to obtain employment is reported it is complete and up to date. For purposes of this paragraph, items of public record relating to arrests, indictments, convictions, suits, tax liens, and outstanding judgments shall be considered up to date if the current public record status of the item at the time of the report is reported.

[15 U.S.C. 1681k. Pub. L. 90–321, 613, as added by Act of Oct. 26, 1970, Pub. L. 91–508, 601, 84 Stat. 1133.]

§ 614 Restrictions on investigative consumer reports

Whenever a consumer reporting agency prepares an investigative consumer report, no adverse information in the consumer report (other than information which is a matter of public record) may be included in a subsequent consumer report unless such adverse information has been verified in the process of making such subsequent consumer report, or the adverse information was received within the three-month period preceding the date the subsequent report is furnished.

[15 U.S.C. 1681l. Pub. L. 90–321, 614, as added by Act of Oct. 26, 1970. Pub. L. 91–508, 601, 84 Stat. 1133.]

§ 615 Requirements on users of consumer reports

(a) Whenever credit or insurance for personal, family, or household purposes, or employment involving a consumer is denied or the charge for such credit or insurance is increased either wholly or partly because of information contained in a consumer report from a consumer reporting agency, the user of the consumer report shall so advise the consumer against whom such adverse action has been taken and supply the name and address of the consumer reporting agency making the report.

(b) Whenever credit for personal, family, or household purposes involving a consumer is denied or the charge for such credit is increased either wholly or partly because of information obtained from a person other than a consumer reporting agency bearing upon the consumer's credit worthiness, credit standing, credit capacity, character, general reputation, personal characteristics, or mode of living, the user of such information shall, within a reasonable period of time, upon the consumer's written request for the reasons for such adverse action received within sixty days after learning of such adverse action, disclose the nature of the information to the consumer. The user of such information shall clearly and accurately disclose to the consumer his right to make such written request at the time such adverse action is communicated to the consumer.

(c) No person shall be held liable for any violation of this section if he shows by a preponderance of the evidence that at the time of the alleged violation he maintained reasonable procedures to assure compliance with the provisions of subsections (a) and (b).

[15 U.S.C. 1681m. Pub. L. 90–321, 615, as added by Act of Oct. 26, 1970, Pub. L. 91–508, 601, 84 Stat. 1133.]

§ 616 Civil liability for willful noncompliance

Any consumer reporting agency or user of information which willfully fails to comply with any requirement imposed under this title with respect to any consumer is liable to that consumer in an amount equal to the sum of:

(1) any actual damages sustained by the consumer as a result of the failure;

(2) such amount of punitive damages as the court may allow; and

(3) in the case of any successful action to enforce any liability under this section, the costs of the action together with reasonable attorney's fees as determined by the court.

[15 U.S.C. 1681n. Pub. L. 90–321, 616, as added by Act of October 26, 1970, Pub. L. 91–508, 601, 84 Stat. 1134.]

§ 617 Civil liability for negligent noncompliance

Any consumer reporting agency or user of information which is negligent in failing to comply with any requirement imposed under this title with respect to any consumer is liable to that consumer in an amount equal to the sum of:

(1) any actual damages sustained by the consumer as a result of the failure;

(2) in the case of any successful action to enforce any liability under this section, the costs of the action together with reasonable attorney's fees as determined by the court.

[15 U.S.C. 1681o. Pub. L. 90–321, 617, as addb by Act of Oct. 26, 1970, Pub. L. 91–508, 601, 84 Stat. 1134.]

§ 618 Jurisdiction of courts; limitation of actions

An action to enforce any liability created under this title may be brought in any appropriate United States district court without regard to the amount in controversy, or in any other court of competent jurisdiction, within two years from the date on which the liability arises, except that where a defendant has materially and willfully misrepresented any information required under this title to be disclosed to an individual and the information so misrepresented is material to the establishment of the defendant's liability to that individual under this title, the action may be brought at any time within two years after discovery by the individual of the misrepresentation.

[15 U.S.C. 1681p. Pub. L. 90–321, 618, as added by Act of Oct. 26, 1970, Pub. L. 91–508, 601, 84 Stat. 1134.]

§ 619 Obtaining information under false pretenses

Any person who knowingly and willfully obtains information on a consumer from a consumer reporting agency under false pretenses shall be fined not more than $5,000 or imprisoned not more than one year, or both.

[15 U.S.C. 1681q. Pub. L. 90–321, 619, as added by Act of Oct. 26, 1970, Pub. L. 91–508, 601, 84 Stat. 1134.]

§ 620 Unauthorized disclosures by officers or employees

Any officer or employee of a consumer reporting agency who knowingly and willfully provides information concerning an individual from the agency's files to a person not authorized to receive that information shall be fined not more than $5,000 or imprisoned not more than one year, or both.

[15 U.S.C. 1681r. Pub. L. 90–321, 620, as added by Act of Oct. 26, 1970, Pub. L. 91–508, 601, 84 Stat. 1134.]

§ 621 Administrative enforcement

(a) Compliance with the requirements imposed under this title shall be enforced under the Federal Trade Commission Act by the Federal Trade Commission with respect to consumer reporting agencies and all other persons subject thereto, except to the extent that enforcement of the requirements imposed under this title is specifically committed to some other government agency under subsection (b) hereof. For the purpose of the exercise by the Federal Trade Commission of its functions and powers under the Federal Trade Commission Act, a violation of any requirement or prohibition imposed under this title shall constitute an unfair or deceptive act or practice in commerce in violation of section 5(a) of the Federal Trade Commission Act and shall be subject to enforcement by the Federal Trade Commission under section 5(b) thereof with respect to any consumer reporting agency or person subject to enforcement by the Federal Trade Commission pursuant to this subsection, irrespective of whether that person is engaged in commerce or meets any other jurisdictional tests in the Federal Trade Commission Act. The Federal Trade Commission shall have such procedural, investigative, and enforcement powers, including the power to issue procedural rules in enforcing compliance with the requirements imposed under this title and to require the filing of reports, the production of documents, and the appearance of witnesses as though the applicable terms and conditions of the Federal Trade Commission Act were part of this title. Any person violating any of the provisions of this title shall be subject to the penalties and entitled to the privileges and immunities provided in the Federal Trade Commission Act as though the applicable terms and provisions thereof were part of this title.

(b) Compliance with the requirements imposed under this title with respect to consumer reporting agencies and persons who use consumer reports from such agencies shall be enforced under:

(1) section 8 of the Federal Deposit Insurance Act, in the case of:

(A) national banks, by the Comptroller of the Currency;

(B) member banks of the Federal Reserve System (other than national banks), by the Federal Reserve Board; and

(C) banks insured by the Federal Deposit Insurance Corporation (other than members of the Federal Reserve System), by the Board of Directors of the Federal Deposit Insurance Corporation.

(2) section 5(d) of the Home Owners Loan Act of 1933, section 407 of the National Housing Act, and sections 6(i) and 17 of the Federal Home Loan Bank Act, by the Federal Home Loan Bank Board (acting directly or through the Federal Savings and Loan Insurance Corporation), in

the case of any institution subject to any of those provisions;

(3) the Federal Credit Union Act, by the Administrator of the National Credit Union Administration with respect to any Federal credit union;

(4) the Acts to regulate commerce, by the Interstate Commerce Commission with respect to any common carrier subject to those Acts;

(5) the Federal Aviation Act of 1958, by the Secretary of Trans-portation with respect to any air carrier or foreign air carrier subject to that Act; and

(6) the Packers and Stockyards Act, 1921 (except as provided in section 406 of the Act), by the Secretary of Agriculture with respect to any activities subject to that Act.

(c) For the purpose of the exercise by any agency referred to in subsection (b) of its powers under any Act referred to in that subsection, a violation of any requirement imposed under this title shall be deemed to be a violation of a requirement imposed under that Act. In addition to its powers under any provision of law specifically referred to in subsection (b), each of the agencies referred to in that subsection may exercise, for the purpose of enforcing compliance with any requirement imposed under this title any other authority conferred on it by law.

[15 U.S.C. 1681s. Pub. L. 90–321, 621, as added by Act of Oct. 26, 1970, Pub. L. 91–508, 601, 84 Stat. 1134; Oct. 3, 1984, Pub. L. 98–443, 98 Stat. 1708.

§ 622 Relation to State laws

This title does not annul, alter, affect, or exempt any person subject to the provisions of this title from complying with the laws of any State with respect to the collection, distribution, or use of any information on consumers, except to the extent that those laws are inconsistent with any provision of this title, and then only to the extent of the inconsistency.

[15 U.S.C. 1681t Pub. L. 90–321, 622, as added by Act of Oct. 26, 1970, Pub. L. 91–508, 601, 84 Stat. 1136.

FAIR CREDIT BILLING ACT

Has the department store's computer ever billed you for merchandise you returned to the store or never received? Or has a credit card company ever charged you twice for the same item or failed to properly credit a payment made on your account? Credit billing errors do occur, but they are easy to resolve if you know how to use the Fair Credit Billing Act (FCBA). Congress passed this law in 1975 to help consumers resolve disputes with creditors and to ensure fair handling of credit accounts.

Which Credit Transactions Are Covered?

The FCBA generally applies only to "open end" credit accounts. Open end accounts include credit cards, revolving charge accounts (such as department store accounts), and overdraft checking. The periodic bills, or billing statements, you receive (usually monthly) for such accounts are covered by the FCBA. The Act does not apply to a loan or credit sale which is paid according to a fixed schedule until the entire amount is paid back.

What Types Of Disputes Are Covered?

The FCBA settlement procedure applies only to disputes over "billing errors" on periodic statements, such as the following:

- Charges not made by you or anyone authorized to use your account.
- Charges which are incorrectly identified or for which the wrong amount or date is shown.
- Charges for goods or services you did not accept or which were not delivered as agreed.
- Computational or similar errors.

- Failure to properly reflect payments or other credits, such as returns.
- Not mailing or delivering bills to your current address (provided you give a change of address at least 20 days before the billing period ends).
- Charges for which you request an explanation or written proof of purchase.

How To Use The Settlement Procedure

When many consumers find a mistake on their bill, they pick up the phone and call the company to correct the problem. You can do this if you wish, but phoning does not trigger the legal safeguards provided under the FCBA.

To be protected under the law, you must send a separate written billing error notice to the creditor. Your notice must reach the creditor within 60 days after the first bill containing the error was mailed to you. Send the notice to the address provided on the bill for billing error notices (and not, for example, directly to the store, unless the bill says that's where it should be sent). In your letter, you must include the following information:

- Your name and account number.
- A statement that you believe the bill contains a billing error and the dollar amount involved.
- The reasons why you believe there is a mistake.

It's a good idea to send it by certified mail, with a return receipt requested. That way you'll have proof of the dates of mailing and receipt. If you wish, send photocopies of sales slips or other documents, but keep the originals for your records.

What Must The Creditor Do?

Your letter claiming a billing error must be acknowledged by the creditor in writing within 30 days after it is received, unless the problem is resolved within that period. In any case, within two billing cycles (but not more than 90 days), the creditor must conduct a reasonable investigation and either correct the mistake or explain why the bill is believed to be correct.

What Happens While A Bill Is Being Disputed?

You may withhold payment of the amount in dispute, including the affected portions of minimum payments and finance charges, until the dispute is resolved. You are still required to pay any part of the bill which is not disputed, including finance and other charges on undisputed amounts.

While the FCBA dispute settlement procedure is going on, the creditor may not take any legal or other action to collect the amount in dispute. Your account may not be closed or restricted in any way, except that the disputed amount may be applied against your credit limit.

What About Your Credit Rating?

While a bill is being disputed, the creditor may not threaten to damage your credit rating or report you as delinquent to anyone. However, the creditor is permitted to report that you are disputing your bill.

Another federal law, the Equal Credit Opportunity Act, prohibits creditors from discriminating against credit applicants who, in good faith, exercise their rights under the FCBA. You cannot be denied credit merely because you have disputed a bill.

If The Creditor Makes A Mistake

If your bill is found to contain a billing error, the creditor must write you explaining the corrections to be made on your account. In addition to crediting your account with the amount not owed, the creditor must remove all finance charges, late fees, or other charges relating to that amount. If the creditor concludes that you owe part of the disputed amount, this must be explained in writing. You also have the right to request copies of documents proving you owe the money.

If The Bill Is Correct

If the creditor investigates and still believes the bill is correct, you must be told promptly in writing how much you owe and why. You may ask for copies of relevant documents. At this point, you will owe the disputed amount, plus any finance charges that accumulated while it was disputed. You may also have to pay the minimum payment amount missed because of the dispute.

If You Still Disagree

Even after the FCBA dispute settlement procedure has ended, you may still feel the bill is wrong. If this happens, write the creditor within 10 days after receiving the explanation and say you still refuse to pay the disputed amount. At this point, the creditor may begin collection procedures. However, if the creditor reports you to a credit bureau as delinquent, he must also state that you don't think you owe the money. Also, you must be told who receives such reports.

If The Creditor Doesn't Follow The Procedures

Any creditor who fails to follow the FCBA dispute settlement procedure may not collect the amount in dispute, or any finance charges on it, up to $50, even if the bill turns out to be correct. For example, this penalty would apply if a creditor acknowledges your complaint in 45 days (15 days too late) or takes more than two billing cycles to resolve a dispute. It also applies if a creditor threatens to report or goes ahead and improperly reports your nonpayments to anyone. You also have the right, as more fully described below, to sue a creditor for any violation of the FCBA.

Complaints About Quality

Disputes about the quality of goods and services are not necessarily "billing errors," so the dispute procedure may not apply. However, if you purchase unsatisfactory goods or services with a credit card, the FCBA allows you to take the same legal actions against the credit card issuer as you could take under state law against the seller. If your state law permits you to withhold payment to a seller for defective merchandise, or pay and sue for a refund, you might also be able to withhold payment to your credit card issuer. Because state laws on your right to stop payment vary, it is best to get legal advice before you do so.

However, before you take legal action, you must give the seller a chance to remedy the problem. Also, unless the seller is also the card issuer (such as a company that issued you a gasoline credit card), you must have bought the item in your home state or within 100 miles of your current mailing address, and the amount charged must have been more than $50.

Other Billing Rights For Consumers

The FCBA also requires "open end" creditors to do the following for their customers:

- Give you a written notice when you open a new account, and at other specified times, describing your right to dispute billing errors.
- Provide a statement for each billing period in which you owe or they owe you more than $1.00.
- Mail or deliver your bill to you at least 14 days before the payment is due, if you are given a time period within which to pay the bill without incurring additional finance or other charges.
- Credit all payments to your account as of the date they are received, unless not doing so would not result in extra charges.
- Promptly credit or refund overpayments.

You Can Also Sue

You can sue a creditor who violates any FCBA provisions. If you win, you may be awarded damages resulting from the violation, plus twice the amount of any finance charges (not less than $100 or more than $1,000). The court may also order the creditor to pay your attorney's fees and costs. If possible, retain a private attorney who is willing to accept whatever fee the court awards as the entire fee for representing you. Some lawyers may not be willing to accept your case unless you agree to pay their fee win or lose or if you will add to a fee awarded by the court but which they believe is too low. Be sure you get a full explanation of what it could cost before you go to court.

Where To Report FCBA Violations

The Federal Trade Commission enforces the FCBA for almost all creditors except banks. While the Commission does not represent individuals in private disputes, information from consumers as to their experiences and concerns is vital to the enforcement of the Act. Questions or complaints may be addressed to the nearest Federal Trade Commission Regional Office. If they concern national creditors, write: Federal Trade Commission, Fair Credit Billing, Washington, D.C. 20580.

915 Second Avenue
SEATTLE, WA 98174
(206) 442–4655

150 Causeway Street
BOSTON, MA 02114
(617) 223–6621

26 Federal Plaza
NEW YORK, NY 10278
(212) 264–1207

118 St. Clair Avenue
CLEVELAND, OH 44114
(216) 522–4207

450 Golden Gate Avenue
SAN FRANCISCO, CA 94102
(415) 556–1270

CENTRAL OFFICE:
6th St. & Pennsylvania Ave.
WASHINGTON, D.C. 20580
(202) 724–1139

55 East Monroe Street
CHICAGO, IL 60603
(312) 353–4423

1405 Curtis Street
DENVER, CO 80202
(303) 837–2271

2001 Bryan Street
DALLAS, TX 75201
(214) 767–0032

11000 Wilshire Boulevard
LOS ANGELES, CA 90024
(213) 824–7575

1718 Peachtree Street, N.W
ATLANTA, GA 30367
(404) 881–4836

FDIC OFFICES

Director
Office of Consumer Affairs & Civil Rights
Federal Deposit Insurance Corp.
Washington, D.C. 20429
(202) 389–4427

ATLANTA REGION Regional Director Federal Deposit Insurance Corp. 233 Peachtree Street, N.E., Suite 2400 Atlanta, GA 30303 (404) 221–6631	 Alabama Florida Georgia
BOSTON REGION Regional Director Federal Deposit Insurance Corp. 60 State Street, 17th Floor Boston, MA 02109 (617) 223–6420	 Connecticut Maine Massachusetts New Hampshire Rhode Island Vermont
CHICAGO REGION Regional Director Federal Deposit Insurance Corp. 233 S. Wacker Drive, Suite 6116 Chicago, IL 60606 (312) 353–2600	 Illinois Indiana
COLUMBUS REGION Regional Director Federal Deposit Insurance Corp. 1 Nationwide Plaza, Suite 2600 Columbus, OH 43215 (614) 469–7301	 Kentucky Ohio West Virginia
DALLAS REGION Regional Director Federal Deposit Insurance Corp.	 Colorado New Mexico

300 North Ervay Street, Suite 3300 Dallas, TX 75201 (214) 754–0098	Oklahoma Texas
KANSAS CITY REGION Regional Director Federal Deposit Insurance Corp. 2345 Grand Avenue, Suite 1500 Kansas City, MO 64108 (816) 374–2851	 Kansas Missouri
MADISON REGION Regional Director Federal Deposit Insurance Corp. 1 South Pinckney Street, Room 813 Madison, WI 53703 (608) 252–5226	 Michigan Wisconsin
MEMPHIS REGION Regional Director Federal Deposit Insurance Corp. 1 Commerce Square, Suite 1800 Memphis, TN 38103 (901) 521–3872	 Arkansas Louisiana Mississippi Tennessee
MINNEAPOLIS REGION Regional Director Federal Deposit Insurance Corp. 730 Second Avenue South, Suite 266 Minneapolis, MN 55402 (612) 725–2046	 Minnesota Montana North Dakota South Dakota Wyoming
NEW YORK REGION Regional Director Federal Deposit Insurance Corp. 345 Park Avenue, 21st Floor New York, NY 10022 (212) 826–4762	 New Jersey New York Puerto Rico Virgin Islands

OMAHA REGION	
Regional Director	Iowa
Federal Deposit Insurance Corp.	Nebraska
1700 Farham Street, Suite 1200	
Omaha, NE 68102	
(402) 221–3366	
PHILADELPHIA REGION	
Regional Director	Delaware
Federal Deposit Insurance Corp.	Maryland
5 Penn Center Plaza, Suite 2901	Pennsylvania
Philadelphia, PA	
(215) 597–2295	
RICHMOND REGION	
Regional Director	District of Columbia
Federal Deposit Insurance Corp.	North Carolina
Eighth and Main Building	South Carolina
707 East Main Street, Suite 2000	Virginia
Richmond, VA 23219	
(804) 782–2395/782–2401	
SAN FRANCISCO REGION	
Regional Director	Alaska, Arizona
Federal Deposit Insurance Corp.	California, Guam
44 Montgomery Street, Suite 3600	Hawaii, Idaho
San Francisco, CA 94104	Nevada, Oregon
(415) 556–2736	Utah, Washington

FEDERAL ENFORCEMENT AGENCIES

National Banks

Comptroller of the Currency
Consumer Affairs Division
Washington, D.C. 20219

State Member Banks

Federal Reserve Bank serving the area in which the State member bank is located.

State Nonmember Banks

FDIC Regional Director for the Region in which the nonmember insured bank is located or the Office of Consumer Affairs and Civil Rights in Washington, D.C. The addresses of these offices are listed in this appendix.

Savings Institutions Insured by the FSLIC and Members of the FHLB System (except for Savings Banks insured by FDIC).

The FHLB's Supervisory Agent in the Federal Home Loan Bank District in which the institution is located.

Federal Credit Unions

Regional Office of the National Credit Union Administration, serving the area in which the Federal Credit Union is located.

Creditors Subject to Civil Aeronautics Board
Director, Bureau of Enforcement

Civil Aeronautics Board
1825 Connecticut Avenue, N.W.
Washington, D.C. 20428

Creditors Subject to Packers and Stockyards Act

Nearest Packers and Stockyards Adminis tration area supervisor.

Federal Land Banks, Federal Land Bank Associations, Federal Intermediate Credit Banks, and Production Credit Associations

Farm Credit Association
490 L'Enfant Plaza West
Washington, D.C. 20578

Retail Department Stores, Consumer Finance Com panies, All Other Creditors, and All Nonbank Credit Card Issuers

Truth in Lending, F.T.C.
Washington, D.C. 20580

FAIR DEBT COLLECTION ACT

If you use credit cards, owe money on a loan, or are paying off a home mortgage, you are a "debtor." Most Americans are. You may never come in contact with a debt collector. But if you do, you should know that there is a law to make sure you are treated fairly. The Fair Debt Collection Practices Act was passed by Congress in 1978 to prohibit certain methods of debt collection. Of course, the law does not erase any legitimate debt you owe. Here are answers to some questions you may have about your rights under the Debt Collection Act:

What Debts Are Covered?

Personal, family, and household debts are covered under the Act. This includes money owed for the purchase of a car, for medical care, or for charge accounts.

Who Is A Debt Collector?

A debt collector is anyone, other than the creditor or the creditor's attorney, who regularly collects debts for others.

How May A Debt Collector Contact You?

A debt collector may contact you in person, by mail, telephone, or telegram. However, a debt collector may not contact you at inconvenient or unusual times or places, such as before 8 a.m. or after 9 p.m. unless you agree. A debt collector may not contact you at work if your employer disapproves.

Can You Stop A Debt Collector From Contacting You?

You may stop a debt collector from contacting you by writing a letter to the collection agency telling them to stop. Once they receive this letter, they may not contact you again except to say there will be no further contact. The debt collector is allowed to notify you that some specific action may be taken, but only if the debt collector or the creditor usually takes such action.

May A Debt Collector Contact Any Other Person Concerning Your Debt?

If you have an attorney, the collector may not contact anyone but the attorney. If you do not have an attorney, a debt collector may contact other people, but only to find out where you live or work. The collector is not allowed to tell anyone other than you or your attorney that you owe money. In most cases, collectors are prohibited from contacting any person more than once.

What Is The Debt Collector Required To Tell You About The Debt?

Within 5 days after you are first contacted, the debt collector must send you a written notice telling you the amount of money you owe; the name of the creditor to whom you owe the money; and what to do if you feel you do not owe the money.

If You Believe You Do Not Owe The Money, May A Debt Collector Continue to Contact You?

The debt collector may not contact you if you send the collector a letter within 30 days after you are first contacted saying you do not owe the money. However, a debt collector can begin collection activities again if you are sent proof of the debt, such as a copy of the bill.

What Types Of Debt Collection Practices Are Prohibited?

Harassment. Debt collectors may not harass, oppress or abuse any person. For example, debt collectors may not:

- Use threats of violence or harm to property or reputation.
- Publish a list of consumers who refuse to pay their debts (except to a credit bureau).
- Use obscene or profane language.
- Repeatedly use the telephone to annoy someone.
- Telephone people without identifying themselves.
- Advertise your debt.

False Statements. Debt collectors may not use anyfalse statements when collecting a debt. For example, debt collectors may not:

- Falsely imply that they are an attorney or government representative.
- Falsely imply that you have committed a crime.
- Falsely represent that they operate or work for a credit bureau.
- Misrepresent the amount of the debt.
- Indicate that papers being sent are legal forms when they are not.
- Indicate that papers being sent are not legal forms when they are.

Also, debt collectors may not say that:

- You'll be arrested if you do not pay your debt.
- They will seize, garnish, attach, or sell your property or wages, unless the collection agency or the creditor intends to do so, and it is legal.

- Actions will be taken against you which legally may not be taken.

Debt collectors may not:

- Give false credit information about you to anyone.
- Send you anything that looks like an official document which might be sent by any court or agency of the United States or any state or local government.
- Use any false name.

Unfair Practices. Debt collectors may not engage in unfair practices in attempting to collect a debt. For example, debt collectors may not:

- Collect any amount greater than your debt, unless allowed by law.
- Deposit a post-dated check before the date on the check.
- Make you accept collect calls or pay for telegrams.
- Take or threaten to take your property unless this can be done legally.
- Contact you by postcard.
- Put anything on an envelope other than the debt collector's address and name. Even the name can't be used if it shows that the communication is about the collection of a debt.

What Control Do You Have Over Specific Debts?

If you owe several debts, any payment you make must be applied to the debt you choose. A debt collector may not apply a payment to any debt you feel you do not owe.

What Can You Do If The Debt Collector Breaks The Law?

You have the right to sue a debt collector in a State or Federal court within one year from the date the law was violated. If you win, you may recover money for the damage you suffered. Court costs and attorney's fees also can be recovered. A group of people may sue a debt collector and recover money for damages up to $500,000.

Who Can You Tell If The Debt Collector Breaks The Law?

In addition to this Federal law, many states have their own debt collection laws. Check with your state Attorney General's office to determine your rights under state law. Federal agencies rely on consumer complaints to decide which companies to investigate. You can assist these enforcement efforts by contacting the appropriate government office.

If a retail store, department store, small loan and finance company, oil company, public utility company, state credit union, government lending program, or travel and expense credit card company is involved, contact the Federal Trade Commission office nearest you:

6th and Pennsylvania, N.W.
WASHINGTON, D.C. 20580
(202) 523–3598

150 Causeway Street
BOSTON, MA 02114
(617) 223–6621

26 Federal Plaza
NEW YORK, NY 10278
(212) 264–1207

118 St. Clair Avenue
CLEVELAND, OH 44114
(216) 522–4207

55 East Monroe Street
CHICAGO, IL 60603
(312) 353–4423

1405 Curtis Street
DENVER, CO 80202
(303) 837–2271

2001 Bryan Street
DALLAS, TX 75201
(214) 767–0032

11000 Wilshire Boulevard
LOS ANGELES, CA 90024
(213) 824–7575

1718 Peachtree Street, N.W.	450 Golden Gate Avenue
ATLANTA, GA 30367	SAN FRANCISCO, CA 94102
(404) 881–4836	(415)556–1270

If your complaint concerns a nationally chartered bank (National or N.A. will be part of the name), write to:

Comptroller of the Currency
Consumer Affairs Division
Washington, D.C. 20219

If your complaint concerns a state chartered bank that is a member of the Federal Reserve System, write to:

Board of Governors of the Federal Reserve System
Consumer Affairs Division
Washington, D.C. 20551

If your complaint concerns a bank that is state chartered and insured by the Federal Deposit Insurance Corporation, but is not a member of the Federal Reserve System, write to:

FDIC
Consumer Affairs Division
Washington, D.C. 20429

If your complaint concerns a federally chartered or federally insured savings and loan association, write to:

Federal Home Loan Bank Board
Washington, D.C. 20552

If your complaint concerns a federally chartered credit union, write to:

National Credit Union Administration
Consumer Affairs Division
Washington, D.C. 20456

EQUAL CREDIT OPPORTUNITY ACT

If you still think only of credit cards when you hear the word "credit," think again. Credit is used by millions of consumers for a variety of purposes: to finance educations, remodel homes, obtain small business loans, and pay for home mortgages.

A law passed by Congress ensures that all consumers will be given an equal chance to receive credit. The Equal Credit Opportunity Act says it is illegal for creditors to discriminate against applicants on the basis of their sex, race, marital status, national origin, religion, age, or because they get public assistance income. This doesn't mean all consumers who apply for credit will get it. Creditors can still use factors such as income, expenses, debts, and credit history to judge applicants.

The law protects you when dealing with any creditor who regularly extends credit, including: banks, small loan and finance companies, retail and department stores, credit card companies, and credit unions. Anyone participating in the decision to grant credit, such as a real estate broker who arranges financing, is covered by the law. Businesses applying for credit are protected by the law, too.

Consumers have equal rights in every phase of the credit application process. Here is a checklist of important rights to remember when you request credit:

When You Apply For Credit, A Creditor May Not...

- Discourage you from applying because of your sex, marital status, age, religion, race, national origin, or because you receive public assistance income.
- Ask you to reveal your sex, race, national origin, or religion. A creditor may ask you to voluntarily disclose this information if you are applying for a real estate loan. This information helps federal

agencies enforce antidiscrimination laws. A creditor may ask what your residence or immigration status is.

- Ask whether you are divorced or widowed.
- Ask what your marital status is if you are applying for a separate, unsecured account. A creditor may ask you to reveal this information if you live in Arizona, California, Idaho, Louisiana, Nevada, New Mexico, Texas, and Washington, the "community property" states. In any state, a creditor may ask for this information if you apply for a joint account or any account secured by property.
- Ask you for information about your husband or wife. A creditor may ask about your spouse if: your spouse is applying with you; your spouse will be allowed to use the account; you are relying on your spouse's income or on alimony or child support income from a former spouse; or if you reside in a community property state (listed above).
- Ask about your plans for having or raising children.
- Ask if you receive alimony, child support, or separate maintenance payments. A creditor may ask for this information if you are first told that you don't have to reveal it if you won't rely on it to get credit. A creditor may ask if you have to pay alimony child support, or separate maintenance payments.

When Deciding To Give You Credit, A Creditor May Not...

- Consider your sex, marital status, race, national origin, or religion.
- Consider whether you have a telephone listing in

your name. A creditor may consider whether there is a phone in your home.

- Consider the race of the people who live in the neighborhood where you want to buy or improve a house with borrowed money.
- Consider your age, with certain exceptions:
- if you are too young to sign contracts. Generally, this applies to those 18 and under.
- if you are 62 or over, and the creditor will favor you because of your age.
- if it is used to determine the meaning of other factors which are important to credit-worthiness. (For example, a creditor could use your age to see if your income might be reduced because you are about to retire.)
- if it is used in a scoring system which favors applicants age 62 and over. A credit-scoring system assigns different points to your answers to application questions. (For example, owning a home might be worth 10 points, while renting might be worth 5.) The total number of points helps the creditor to decide if you are credit-worthy.

When Evaluating Your Income, A Creditor May Not...

- Refuse to consider reliable public assistance income in the same manner as other income.
- Discount income because of your sex or marital status. (For example, a creditor cannot count a man's salary at 100% and a woman's at 75%.) A creditor may not assume a woman of child bearing age will stop work to have or raise children.
- Discount or refuse to consider income because it

is derived from part-time employment or from pension, annuity, or retirement benefit programs.

- Refuse to consider consistently received alimony, child support, or separate maintenance payments. A creditor may ask you for proof that this income has been received consistently.

You Also Have The Right...

- To have credit in your maiden name (Mary Smith), your first name and your husband's last name (Mary Jones), or your first name and a combined last name (Mary Smith-Jones).
- To get credit without a co-signer, if you meet the creditor's standards.
- To have a co-signer other than your husband or wife, if one is necessary.
- To keep your own accounts after you change your name, marital status, reach a certain age, or retire, unless the creditor has evidence that you are unable or unwilling to pay.
- To know whether your application was accepted or rejected within 30 days of filing it.
- To know why your application was rejected. The creditor must either immediately give you the specific reasons for your rejection or tell you of your right to learn the reasons if you ask them within 60 days. (Examples of reasons are: "Your income was too low," or "You haven't been employed at your job long enough." Examples of unaccept able reasons are: "You didn't meet our minimum standards," or "You didn't receive enough points on our credit scoring system.") Indefinite and vague reasons are illegal, ask for specifics.

- To learn the specific reasons why you were offered less favorable terms than you applied for. (Examples of less favorable terms include higher finance charges or less money than you requested). This does not hold if you accept the less favorable terms.
- To know the specific reasons why your account was closed or why the terms of the account were made less favorable to you. This does not hold if these actions were taken because your account was delinquent or because you have not used the account for some time.

A Special Note To Women

A good credit history, or record of how you paid past bills is often necessary to obtain credit. Unfortunately, this hurts many married, separated, divorced, and widowed women. There are two common reasons women do not have credit histories in their own names: they lost their credit histories when they married and changed their name, and creditors reported accounts shared by married couples in the husband's name only.

The law says that when creditors report histories to credit bureaus or to other creditors they must report information on accounts shared by married couples in both names. This is true only for accounts opened after June 1, 1977. If you and your spouse opened an account before that time, you should ask the creditor to use both names.

If you are married, divorced, separated, or widowed, you should make a special point to call or visit your local credit bureau(s) to ensure that all relevant information is in a file under your own name. To learn more about building your credit file, write for a free brochure,

"Women and Credit Histories," from any of the FTC offices listed below.

What You Can Do If You Suspect Discrimination...

- Complain to the creditor. Make it known that you are aware of the law. The creditor may reverse the decision or detect an error.
- Many states have their own equal credit opportunity laws. Check with your state's Attorney General's office to see if the creditor violated state laws. Your state may decide to take the creditor to court.
- Bring a case in Federal district court. If you win, you can recover actual damages and be awarded a penalty. You can also recover reasonable attorney's fees and court costs. An attorney can advise you on how to proceed.
- Join with others to file a class action suit. You may recover punitive damages for the class of up to $500,000 or 1% of the creditor's net worth, whichever is less.
- Report violations to the appropriate government agency. If you are denied credit, the creditor must give you the name and address of the agency to contact. While the agencies do not resolve individual complaints, they do use consumer comments to decide which companies to investigate.

Where To Send Complaints And Questions

If a retail store, department store, small loan and finance company, oil company, public utility company, state credit union, government lending program, or travel and expense company is involved, contact the Federal Trade Commission office nearest you:

915 Second Avenue
SEATTLE, WA 98174
(206) 442–4655

150 Causeway Street
BOSTON, MA 02114
(617) 223–6621

26 Federal Plaza
NEW YORK, NY 10278
(212) 264–1207

118 St. Clair Avenue
CLEVELAND, OH 44114
(216) 522–4207

450 Golden Gate Avenue
SAN FRANCISCO, CA 94102
(415) 556–1270

55 East Monroe Street
CHICAGO, IL 60603
(312) 353–4423

1405 Curtis Street
DENVER, CO 80202
(303) 837–2271

8303 Elmbrook Drive
DALLAS, TX 75247
(214) 767–7050

11000 Wilshire Boulevard
LOS ANGELES, CA 90024
(213) 209–7575

1718 Peachtree Street, N.W.
ATLANTA, GA 30367
(404) 881–4836

CENTRAL OFFICE:
6th St. and Washington Ave.
WASHINGTON, D.C. 20580
(202) 523–3598

If your complaint concerns a nationally chartered bank (National or N.A. will be part of the name), write to:

Comptroller of the Currency
Consumer Affairs Division
Washington, D.C. 20219

If your complaint concerns a state chartered bank that is a member of the Federal Reserve System, write to:

Board of Governors of the Federal Reserve System
Consumer Affairs Division
Washington, D.C. 20551

If your complaint concerns a bank that is state chartered and insured by the Federal Deposit Insurance Corporation, but is not a member of the Federal Reserve System, write to:

FDIC
Consumer Affairs Division
Washington, D.C. 20429

If your complaint concerns a federally chartered or federally insured savings and loan association, write to:

Federal Home Loan Bank Board
Equal Credit Opportunity
Washington, D.C. 20552

If your complaint concerns a federally chartered credit union, write to:

National Credit Union Administration
Consumer Affairs Division,
Washington, D.C. 20456

Complaints against all kinds of creditors can be referred to:

Department of Justice
Civil Rights Division
Washington, D.C. 20530

GLOSSARY

ANNUAL FEE: Anytime you receive a new credit card, especially so with the major credit cards, you will be charged a set fee usually around twenty bucks for the privileges of having and using the card. And if you want to have this credit card the following year, your account will be charged the annual fee for the next 12 months for usage of the card. If you're against the idea of paying an annual fee, contact Bankcard Holders of America and purchase their list of credit card issuers with No Annual Fees.

BAD CHECK PASSERS: This is a person who knows full well, in advance, that the check he's trying to cash or use in a transaction is either fake, stolen or not covered by the funds in his account. Another term used in the industry is a Paperhanger, and the prisions are loaded with them.

BAIT AND SWITCH: A good example for this is when you're looking for a new car and come across an advertisement that has just what you want, at an "unbelievable" price. The next thing you do is rush down to the dealership who ran the ad, only to have a salesman tell you that "the car you want has been sold"—"but come right over here and look at this here little gem" and of course it's overpriced and it looks like hell. They pull you in on half-priced lobster and then try to sell you on a TV dinner.

BILL COLLECTOR: It's the person who calls your home just as you sit down to eat your Bait and switch TV dinner and rags on you over the settlement or partial payment of a past-due account.

B-K: An abbreviated term for Bankruptcy.

BLACK BALL: A term used in the credit industry to say that a customer or debter has been "cut-off" or Black

Balled from any further credit privileges.

BLOCK GRANT PROGRAM: This is generally a Housing and Urban Development (HUD) program that has targeted a specific area or neighborhood for redevelopment or upgrades. Moneis have already been set aside and anyone who owns or wants to buy a home in the target area can apply for a grant to make the improvements. Being it's "grant money," you need not pay it back; they may pay all the expenses in your project or match you dollar for dollar.

BOGUS FINANCIAL STATEMENTS: Documents used for loans and lines of credit usually involving a business loan, which have been altered or made up of misleading information and figures.

BUM CHECKS: Checks that are probably not even worth the paper they're printed on.

CASH SOCIETY: A society made up of consumers and merchants who generally paid for their goods and services with "cash" money: The opposite of a "Credit Society."

CHECKS COME MARCHING HOME: Here's where you've written several checks to pay bills and buy things with and later find out (once the checks have come marching home) that your spouse "forgot" to deposit or transfer funds into your checking account and now here they all come, with a $15 N.S.F. fee on each.

COLLATERAL: Consumers pledge their new car as collateral when getting an auto loan. Homebuyers pledge the home they're about to purchase as collateral when getting a home loan. Anything of "value" can be considered "collateral," it's used to "secure" a lenders position in a loan. If you default on the loan, the lender then sells your collateral to help recover the money you borrowed.

CONSUMER DISPUTES: Usually a written request by a consumer, to a credit bureau stating that there's inaccurate information contained in the consumer file that he wants corrected.

CONSUMER REPORT: A formal name for "Credit Report."

CONTRACTUAL LIABILITY: The legal garb, found mostly in contracts concerning some form of credit that makes you "liable" to pay off a debt. As a co-signer, you are contractually liable for paying off a loan if the primary or first party (the one you co-signed for) does'nt make the payments.

COVER YOUR ASS-ETS: Another way of saying "duck!" It's a protection measure taken advantage of by individuals who don't want to be taken advantage of by a potential adversary or lawsuit.

CREDIT CARD PUSHERS: A "very aggressive" bank or financial institution that is trying to cash-in on the huge profits earned on credit card interest rates.

CREDIT CHECK-UP: It's something you do at least once a year, making sure that your credit reports are accurate, up to date and clear of any derogatory remarks.

CREDIT PROFILE: A compilation of credit reports containing information about you from all of the major credit bureaus in your state or region.

CREDIT REPORTING AGENCY: Another term for "Credit Bureau."

CREDIT REPORTING BUREAU: Another term for "Credit Bureau."

CREDIT SOCIETY: A society made up of individuals who use credit cards and lines of credit, to purchase things they can't afford: The opposite of a "cash society."

CREDIT UNION: The best bet in town generally to establish a long term banking relationship with: A cooperative organization that makes low-interest loans to its members.

DEAD BEAT: A person who does not make good on his debts.

DEBIT CARD: A credit card that debits your account while crediting a merchants account. All transactions are subject to having enough money in your account to cover any particular purchase.

DEBT SERVICE: A term used by lenders when referring to a persons' ability to "service" or pay the payments of a debt.

DEFAULT: Failure to fulfill an obligation.

DETRIMENT: To damage.

ENTREPRENEUR: Any person who launches a business venture, assuming all risks for sake of profit.

FINANCE COMPANY: A financial institution who makes consumer credit loans, often times taking greater risks and therefore charging high rates of interest.

FORECLOSURE: The termination of a mortgage loan agreement, taking legal possession of the property.

FORMAL ASSUMPTION: To assume an existing mortgage; becoming contractually liable for the repayment of the loan.

FRIVOLOUS: Trivial, insignificant.

HIGH PRIESTS IN HOLY TEMPLES: A description of bankers who think they're God and their skyscrapers are Heaven.

HIGH ROLLER: If when you talk about money, E F Hutton and bank presidents listen, then you are one, providing you're not a federal auditor or regulator.

INQUIRY: The recordation of any attempt made by a lender or merchant seeking to acquire credit information about you from a credit bureau.

INFINITY CARD: A Visa or Mastercard processed by a bank or credit card company that bears the name of a national organization, which is issued only to its members.

JUDGEMENT: The decision reached by a court that you owe, and are to pay whatever amount is awarded by the judge, to the plantiff or creditor.

LIEN: The legal right to take and hold or sell the property of another to satisfy an obligation or debt.

LOAN PACKAGE: All the documents that a lender will require to evaluate and make a mortgage or business loan.

LOAN SHARK: A person who is financed and supported by gangsters. Some finance companies fall into this group (less the gangsters).

"NO QUESTION ASKED" LINE OF CREDIT: A line of credit that requires nothing more than a signature and a few minutes of your time before walking out with the money.

N.S.F. stands for "Non Sufficient Funds," meaning you are short on your checking account balance if you start getting these notices in the mail.

PLASTIC PURSUIT: The race among banks, thrifts and other pushers to get their credit card into the market place before a competitor does.

PROCEEDS: The money you end up with after the closing of a business transaction.

PUBLIC RECORDS: Liens, judgements, bankruptcy filings and notices of default are all a matter of public record at your local City Hall. They can be viewed by the general public or any individual wishing to view them for business purposes. The credit bureau hires a service (many use a firm called Statewide) that does nothing but search for new filings, this is how liens, judgements and bankruptcy information gets back to the credit bureau and stored for future use.

REMAIN BLOWING IN THE WIND: A check that remains outstanding after it has been processed by the bank twice. The final result of a Paperhangers efforts. (See Bad Check Passers).

REPO MAN: The person a bank hires to come out and steal your car.

REPO ORDER: The paperwork giving the Repo-man, a license to steal your car.

ROBBING PETER TO PAY PAUL: A form commonly used to juggle bills.

ROB THE BANK WITHOUT A GUN: The act of getting a loan and never paying it back.

SAVINGS AND LOAN: The financial institution that is going to cost Americans "billions" of dollars to bail out.

SCREWS: (*See Black Ball*).

SECURED CREDIT LINE: Any credit line which is backed by collateral.

SHORTY APPLICATION: A short form credit application usually provided by credit card pushers.

SILENT BUMP: A process for increasing your credit card limit without having to re-apply for it.

SLIPPERY DUDES: Con Man posing as a salesperson.

STRAW BUYER: Another form of "Co-signer."

STRONG ARMS COLLECTION AGENCY: The firm who employs the idiot who calls you at all un-godly hours seeking a payment on your past due account.

THRIFT: Another term used for a Savings and Loan institution.

UNSECURED CREDIT LINE: A credit line not backed by collateral.

VERY SHARP COOKIE: One who reads through this book a second time.

INDEX

INDEX